Praise for *Trauma-Informed Spiritual Care*

This book meets many needs as a textbook for spiritual care courses and clinical training for chaplains and religious leaders in any tradition. It focuses on the unique ways that spiritual caregivers can use a narrative approach to trauma care based upon Judith Herman's time-honored process of helping survivors practice safety, remembrance, mourning, and meaning-making. Its accessible language builds upon scholarship in pastoral care and research about the impact of trauma on the body and spiritual struggles. It describes a step-by-step approach that caregivers will want to return to over and over again in spiritual care of trauma.

—Carrie Doehring, Clifford Baldridge Professor of Pastoral Care and Counseling, Iliff School of Theology

The day before I opened *Trauma-Informed Spiritual Care*, I replayed the traumatic last minutes of my father's life, and grief took up residence in my heart. Danielle Tumminio Hansen's book gave me new language to reconnect with self, life-giving rituals to mourn, and theoretical frameworks to salve my healing wound. For this resource that moved me from head to heart, I am grateful. I give thanks that care seekers, therapists, and spiritual caregivers who pick up this book will take a similar journey.

—Gregory C. Ellison II, executive director of Fearless Dialogues, and associate professor of transformative leadership and communal care, Emory University's Candler School of Theology

Trauma-Informed Spiritual Care is an insightful, readable, and practical text that provides deep wisdom through accessible prose. Danielle Tumminio Hansen has written a gem of a book, ideal for courses on spiritual care, for CPE reading lists, for chaplains, religious and lay leaders, and others who seek to expand their capacity for spiritual care. Her invitational narrative style and easeful integration of theory and practice offer examples and case studies, activities and diagrams to

help readers understand the effects of trauma and how spiritual care can support the journey to healing and justice.

—Pamela R. McCarroll, Jane and Geoffrey Martin Chair in Practical Theology, Emmanuel College, Victoria University in the University of Toronto

This is a much-needed, deeply informed, accessible resource for guiding spiritual care providers privileged to walk beside survivors of trauma. Tumminio Hansen skillfully interweaves theoretical and clinical guidance that chaplains and parish clergy alike will be able to engage and employ. Importantly, she illustrates how experiences of embedded oppression, such as racism and sexism, amplify other forms of trauma and must inform practices of restorative justice and care. I highly commend this resource for MDiv and DMin classrooms and for ACPE, VA, and military chaplaincy training programs.

—Nancy J. Ramsay, director of the Soul Repair Center, and professor emerita of pastoral theology and care, Brite Divinity School, Fort Worth, Texas

Trauma-Informed Spiritual Care

Trauma-Informed Spiritual Care

Interventions for Safety, Meaning, Reconnection, and Justice

Danielle Tumminio Hansen

FORTRESS PRESS
Minneapolis

TRAUMA-INFORMED SPIRITUAL CARE
Interventions for Safety, Meaning, Reconnection, and Justice

Portions of chapter 5 were originally published as "Restorative Justice and Pastoral Care: Shared Principles and Practices" by Danielle Tumminio Hansen in *Journal of Pastoral Theology*, February 6, 2024. Reprinted with permission.

29 28 27 26 25 24 1 2 3 4 5 6 7 8 9

Library of Congress Cataloging-in-Publication Data

Names: Tumminio, Danielle Elizabeth, author.
Title: Trauma-informed spiritual care : interventions for safety, meaning, reconnection, and justice / Danielle Tumminio Hansen.
Description: Minneapolis : Fortress Press, [2024] | Includes bibliographical references and index.
Identifiers: LCCN 2024000049 (print) | LCCN 2024000050 (ebook) | ISBN 9781506485836 (print) | ISBN 9781506485843 (ebook)
Subjects: LCSH: Psychic trauma--Religious aspects. | Psychology, Religious.
Classification: LCC BL65.M45 T86 2024 (print) | LCC BL65.M45 (ebook) | DDC 259/.418--dc23/eng/20240308
LC record available at https://lccn.loc.gov/2024000049
LC ebook record available at https://lccn.loc.gov/2024000050

Cover image: Stock photograph by Scharvik from Getty Images
Cover design: Marti Naughton

Print ISBN: 978-1-5064-8583-6
eBook ISBN: 978-1-5064-8584-3

To my students,
and to those who seek answers

CONTENTS

ACKNOWLEDGMENTS

When I entered academia, I hoped to make a difference in the lives of students but also to continue to be a student myself. The instinct to learn remains fundamental to my sense of identity and call, and I am profoundly indebted to the other pastoral theologians in my field who are likewise determined to enrich what they know so that they can synthesize and share it with others. They model curiosity, wisdom, altruism, and amity, and one of the great blessings in my life is to be able to call them colleagues and friends. I owe particular thanks to the anonymous peer reviewers who read the entirety of this book and offered insightful feedback, as well as to Carrie Doehring, Kristen Leslie, Pam McCarroll, and Mindy McGarrah Sharp, who always welcomed conversations about the project.

In addition to these scholars, I am grateful for insights on attachment theory from my colleague Geoff Goodman, as well as the camaraderie and wisdom of fellow pastoral theologians Greg Ellison and Emmanuel Lartey, all of whom work with me at Emory University. Justin Fannon provided detailed and timely research assistance on this project, while students in my trauma and theology classes at both the Seminary of the Southwest and Emory University helped me understand the need for a book like this.

I am profoundly grateful to have had the chance to work with Carey Newman and the team at Fortress Press. They provided exemplary editorial and publication support throughout.

Finally, I extend my thanks to my family, who teach me every day about joy and love.

PREFACE

Pervasive and persistent, trauma transmits across the lifespan, across communities, and across generations. It possesses the strength to destroy one's sense of safety and purpose, to challenge one's meaning-making capacities and relationships, striking at unexpected times that, in turn, ravage closely guarded assumptions of agency and belief. Providing fodder for theodicy, trauma poses significant challenges to theologians, probing them to justify how the world can house God alongside such horrors. Indeed, people of faith, like Job, may be left begging for answers or a way forward that allows them to regain a sense that life can be good overall, that there is something beyond the negative event or events that brought them to their knees.[1]

Having spent more than a decade studying how trauma affects humans, I remain convinced that understanding its nuances is essential for spiritual care providers, who often find themselves engaging with the muck and mire of trauma's aftermath. That muck and mire can affect a person physically, existentially, spiritually, cognitively, and emotionally. In other words, trauma can and often does affect a person's whole self. The spiritual caregiver thus needs an understanding of trauma that includes the whole self, which I seek to provide in what follows.

In addition, they must understand the unique role they can play in the healing process. Spiritual caregivers must simultaneously recognize the limits of their expertise—for they are neither doctor nor therapist—while acknowledging the important contributions they can make. This book seeks to parse out this important topic as well, exploring how spiritual care providers can be transformational resources when they employ their gifts.

Reading about spiritual care can be a thought-provoking experience. It can cause the reader to think about their own faith background and their current beliefs. In addition, it may be challenging to be exposed to the suffering that trauma imposes—even from the distance provided by the written word—given how empathic spiritual caregivers tend to be. You may remember prior experiences of trauma. There may be material in the book that triggers or upsets you. If this is the case, please stop reading and seek out appropriate support and body-centered spiritual self-care practices. The book will be here for you when you are ready to return to it. All too often, caregivers neglect their own needs because they believe they must do so to care for others, but this kind of work isn't sustainable if caregivers don't recognize and attend to their own wellness. Practicing self-care is one way to promote personal wellness and avoid exhaustion, burnout, and the infliction of harm onto care seekers. Seeking out support is another. I encourage you to do both, not only as you read this book, but also as you engage in the art of spiritual care on the whole.

Spiritual caregiving is only as relevant as it is able to engage with the reality of people's lives. Trauma is part of that reality, part of the sometimes beautiful and sometimes awful world in which we live. To equip caregivers with the knowledge and skills to engage with trauma's aftermath is therefore to equip caregivers with the knowledge and skills to help people transcend and integrate suffering. In so doing, caregivers offer both hope and healing. They help to transition trauma from an ongoing reality to a memory in people's lives, so that care seekers can step forward into a future filled not with anguish but with stability, understanding, and solidarity.

INTRODUCTION

Imagine a world where clouds never materialize, where every person—old and young—eats cupcakes for breakfast with no fear of clogging arteries or spiking blood sugar. Imagine a world with no violence, no lies, no suffering, and perhaps—boldly—no death. In this world, trauma doesn't exist or, perhaps, is reminisced as a distant story instead of a reality.

This is not the world we live in.

Case in point: a study conducted in twenty-four countries found that over 70 percent of adults had experienced at least one event that the psychological community considers a likely precursor to developing **post-traumatic stress disorder** (PTSD).[1] The United States tied for third in that list of twenty-four—the South American nation of Columbia was its partner—with 82.7 percent of individuals reporting at least one such event in their lives.[2] Only Peru and Ukraine presented higher rates. To nuance that domestic data a little, the Centers for Disease Control estimates that 61 percent of adults in the United States lived through at least one potentially traumatic event (also called an "Adverse Childhood Event") by the time they were eighteen, and one in six adults had experienced four or more potentially traumatic events. That same study found that five of the ten leading causes of death are linked to exposure from such events and that reducing the number of potentially traumatic events a person experiences in childhood could reduce lifetime rates of depression by 44 percent.[3]

Trauma, in other words, is not an illusion, nor is it an abstraction. It happens not rarely but regularly, hauntingly, and with devastating effects upon individuals and communities. It is neither rare nor exotic.

It is pervasive, and it has a profound effect on the lives of individuals and communities. Spiritual care providers need skills to understand trauma's nuances and resources to counter its effects. They also need resources for thinking about trauma theologically and spiritually alongside targeted interventions for care. What follows provides some of those resources.

One of the cornerstone assertions of all that lies ahead is that relationships matter. People of faith are often people of who recognize that. They know that humans need one another, that God uses the concrete reality of this world to offer glimpses—sometimes even shadows—of hope. However, the rich comfort of relationships is something that trauma tends to thieve away. Trauma often robs people of their communities, leaving them feeling isolated and afraid. But the isolated feeling that accompanies trauma doesn't mean that trauma is only an individual event. Indeed, traumas that seem to be individual are often collective, emerging from a community and affecting a community. There are also traumas that are more clearly collective—as the Covid-19 pandemic, the climate crisis, and systemic injustices like racism and sexism show—but which affect individuals.

The way people exist together, in other words, is both humanity's greatest strength and the basis for the greatest harms we inflict upon one another. Spiritual caregivers, therefore, need to understand not only how trauma works individually but also how it moves horizontally across communities and vertically across generations in ways that can be insidious and go unnamed and unaddressed.

Because trauma recovery requires safety and stability, an overview of the book is provided for a grounded reading experience. The first chapter offers an examination of trauma from multiple perspectives—physically, psychologically, spiritually, and narratively. From there, chapters 2 to 4 utilize Judith Herman's threefold framework for healing to explore how spiritual caregivers can think about and help survivors practice safety, remembrance, mourning, meaning-making, and reconnection. Chapter 5 examines how restorative justice can be an effective resource for spiritual caregivers who are helping survivors of trauma. I utilize the terms "spiritual care" and "pastoral care" interchangeably, recognizing that there is nuance between them. I also use the terms "spiritual caregiver" or "pastoral caregiver" to refer to someone trained in the art of offering support in the form of pastoral care. Such individuals include ordained ministers as well as chaplains and lay individuals who have completed appropriate training, which may include a graduate degree like a master of divinity or units of Clinical Pastoral Education (CPE).

A few limitations of note: While this book touches upon core competencies, it is not primarily focused on teaching them, primarily because experts in spiritual care have so effectively done this work elsewhere.[4] In addition, this book does not focus upon caregiving with children, although chapter 1 does include a discussion of the signs and symptoms of trauma in children so that caregivers can help them find appropriate support. While my hope is that this book may be of use cross-culturally, it focuses primarily upon trauma as constructed and researched within Western contexts. Finally, readers benefit from scholars who are transparent about who they are and what they bring to the table, both in terms of their commitments and their background. I am a white, middle class, cisgender woman who is ordained as an Episcopal priest and a faculty member at a major research university. I come from a family with extensive lived experience of disability, as my father passed away from a battle with ALS (Lou Gehrig's Disease) that lasted close to twenty years. As a young adult, I experienced a rape that caused significant psychological distress and was one of the reasons why I became interested in trauma and spiritual care as a field of study.[5] I have also trusted others who helped me spiritually integrate prior experiences of suffering. Like all scholars, I bring my life experiences to my research in ways of which I am sometimes aware and sometimes not.

Trauma is one of the most pervasive of human experiences, just as it is an experience that affects the whole self of those who live through it. Spiritually, trauma can pose unique and sometimes lonely challenges. Receiving spiritual support from someone trustworthy who understands how trauma works can therefore be both grounding and life-giving in a way that helps people to spiritually integrate the perpetual presence of trauma in life-giving ways.

CHAPTER ONE

Introduction to Trauma

I WAS WALKING down the sidewalk of a large city around three thirty in the afternoon. It was late spring, the time of year when flowers have already sprouted from the ground but the weather hadn't become saturated with heat and humidity. Across the street, the doors of a high school opened as a loud bell sounded and students spilled out of the confines of the building and into the open air.

"That test was totally traumatic," I heard one student say to another, slinging a backpack over her shoulder.

"Totally," said the other. "I have so much PTSD now."

I raised an eyebrow as they walked away, thinking about how common it has become to talk about trauma this way—casually and nonchalantly, as a synonym for "overwhelming" instead of a unique form of suffering. In some ways, this is progress, a positive step forward in terms of recognizing when stress overwhelms one's capacity to cope, especially in the oft all-or-nothing worldview of an adolescent. And yet, the way in which terms like "trauma" and "PTSD" have become commonplace raises another set of questions: What exactly *is* PTSD? Moreover, what constitutes trauma and how is it different from other forms of suffering? What follows explores and answers these questions.

What is Trauma?

It might seem as if traumas should be easy to identify—they're just the worst kind of things, right? If only it were so simple. Trauma is difficult to identify because it is difficult to quantify. Indeed, there is no objective criteria for a traumatic event, no list that a person can draw up in order to check a box. Instead, trauma is a matter of perception. Put differently, what makes an event traumatic is how a person reacts to it.

Before explaining what trauma is, then, it is helpful to explain what trauma is *not*. Trauma is different from **stress**. Stress occurs when a person feels they cannot meet the demands of their environment.[1] Like trauma, there is no objective criteria for what constitutes stress. Instead, stress is defined by a person's perception of their environment, such that what might be stressful for one person might not be stressful for another. (Imagine a person who cannot swim being asked to swim a lap versus an Olympic swimmer being asked to swim a lap, and you get the point).

It is also helpful to note here that not all stress causes distress. For instance, a person who is preparing to take a theology test may feel stressed by everything that they must learn for the exam. However, they may also be aware that they *can* remember everything, especially because they take excellent notes and have been rereading them after each class. So even though the hypothetical person feels stressed, they are not overwhelmed, sad, or anxious about it. In contrast, imagine another student who is studying for the same test but who skipped class several times and was texting on their phone during lectures. This student also feels stress about the upcoming exam but is anxious because they know they do not have the resources to pass. As a result, this student feels distress that the other student does not.

The difference between a stress and a trauma is the degree to which the person is overwhelmed by it. Whereas a stress taxes an individual's coping mechanisms, a trauma overwhelms them. Here is a helpful definition of trauma to help clarify what it is: A **trauma** is a highly distressing event or series of events that occurs in the life of an individual or community and which overwhelms their capacity to cope, often because of a sense of threat to their lives and what is most meaningful to them.

Some of the life-threatening characteristics of potentially traumatic events may be easier to identify. Other overwhelming experiences may carry a sense of threat that may be more difficult to name because the threat feels insidious or because society does not appear to label them as overwhelming. For instance, it may be traumatic for a child to switch from one school to another, especially if they have to move to a new town and make all new friends. Such an event may disrupt and even threaten a child's sense of stability and make them feel afraid, unsafe, or unloved.

Now, one might respond by saying, "But children switch schools all the time!" or "Well, I switched schools as a child, and that wasn't my experience." These reactions illustrate two different kinds of fallacies when it comes to trauma. The first is that trauma is rare. Mental health professionals *used* to believe that trauma was rare; indeed, they thought trauma was primarily limited to instances of combat. But beginning in the latter half of the 1900s, mental health professionals like Judith Herman began to question that assumption. Herman recognized that sexual violations often resulted in trauma reactions and that such events were not rare but rather were a common part of human existence.[2] Indeed, as stated in the introduction, mental health leaders now recognize that a majority of people experience trauma at some point in their lives.

The second fallacy about trauma is that all events are experienced the same way by all people. This is rarely the case. Individuals often interpret events differently due to several factors, including prior experiences, resiliency, social support, age, beliefs, and so forth.[3] In other words, we bring our whole selves to the processing of our experiences, and because each of us is different, we each process experiences in different ways. Thus, two individuals may well have the same or similar experiences and interpret them differently. Also, having trustworthy relationships for coping with trauma is one of the crucial factors in whether or not an acute experience of stress results, over time, in post-traumatic symptoms. This is especially true if trauma generates spiritual struggles.[4]

As a result of the distinctions between individuals and the resources they can access, it becomes difficult to label events themselves as "traumatic." Instead, what turns an event from "potentially traumatic" to "traumatic" is the process of interpretating it and the help people have in that process. This is not to say that a negative event like an attempted murder or a rape or a hurricane is potentially morally neutral or morally beneficial if the individuals involved did not have a trauma reaction (although it's hard to imagine they would not). Such events are negative no matter how we interpret them. For it to be considered a trauma, however, the individual must experience a certain amount of distress—at least in the short-term.

Trauma as Physiological

It is impossible to discuss trauma without discussing the body because the body is where trauma is experienced, housed, and processed over time. Indeed, as Bessel van der Kolk summarizes, the body keeps the score when it comes to traumatic experiences. One of the reasons why trauma gets experienced this way is because of the role that **adrenaline** plays in trauma. Adrenaline is both a hormone and a neurotransmitter that is manufactured by the adrenal gland and is essential to the body's **fight, flight, or freeze** response (also known as an **acute stress response**). Many traumatized individuals experience a rise in adrenaline because the body perceives the trauma as a threat and goes into fight, flight, or freeze to respond to it. After the trauma is over, the adrenaline may not return to its normal levels or may spike more easily than it did before. This results in sleep problems, irritability, and problems with attention and memory.[5]

Traumatized individuals also may have overactivity in the part of the brain known as the **amygdala**, especially when presented with information that reminds them of the trauma. The amygdala activates the body's stress response and warns the body of danger. Heightened levels of activity in the amygdala can lead to a state of physiological arousal marked by an increase in heart rate, oxygen levels, and blood pressure. But while the levels of activity in the amygdala may be heightened when a traumatized person is reminded of the event, there is a corresponding decrease in activity in **Broca's area**, the region of the brain responsible for language. As a result, individuals who are traumatized and who reexperience traumatic memories during flashbacks may struggle to speak about the event because this part of the brain is inactive. This can make it difficult for traumatized individuals to talk, even as they may simultaneously have heightened physical flashbacks of the trauma.

In other words, the event is simultaneously able to be evoked but beyond language. This is one reason why the body reexperiences the trauma in flashbacks and nightmares—when a person cannot tell the story of the trauma, the body tells it for them.[6]

Finally, if left unmanaged, trauma reorganizes how the right and left sides of the brain work together. Ordinarily, the two sides of the brain act in tandem with one another, almost as neurological dance partners. The right side of the brain handles emotion, space, feeling, and intuition while the left side takes care of executive functioning, language, and logic, and can recall concrete data, like facts relating to an event. In traumatized individuals, the left side of the brain becomes less active, meaning that individuals struggle with creating plans, organizing experiences, or creating sequences of events.[7]

It has become common to encourage traumatized individuals to talk about their experiences in order to process them. But while talking can be helpful, people need to feel safe before they can benefit from talking, which is why initially they need help with some of the physiological symptoms of trauma. Mental health professionals are well-aware of the need to engage the whole self—including the body—in trauma recovery, and therapeutic interventions including eye movement desensitization and reprocessing (EMDR) and yoga have been shown to be particularly helpful because they help people learn how to cope with the body-based aftermath of trauma. As I'll elaborate in later chapters, spiritual caregivers also have resources they can draw upon to help care seekers process trauma not just with their minds or their words but also with their bodies.

Trauma as Narrative

Humans are embodied stories, fundamentally narrative from the start. They tell stories about themselves as well as about their friends, family, and communities to make sense of who they are and the world that they live in. This is not something they can do in isolation for several reasons. First, humans are directly involved in writing the narrative of their lives. Indeed, they are storied from the start, and they write that story in conjunction with others. When they're born, they're born into a family and a culture that already has a set of stories, and they become a part of those to a varying extent. For instance, I was born into a family that is Italian on both sides, and being Italian was an important part of who I was told I was as a young child. My parents and grandparents imparted this part of my story through the food we ate, the celebrations we had, the religion we practiced, and the Italian curse words that my grandma sprinkled into conversations. Being Italian, in other words, wasn't something I chose to be in my 20s or 30s. It was part of the story that I inherited when I was born, almost as if, at birth, I stepped into a flowing river and was swept along with the current.

This is an example of how caregivers oftentimes become the first people who construct the stories of an infant's life, because they're too young to do so. But as that child gets older and more able to construct their narrative, it still isn't an individual enterprise. Instead, their friends, chosen family, and the wider community continue to play a role in that process. They may do so by being involved in pivotal events in a person's life that become essential to their stories. But they may also do so in more casual, more ordinary ways. Here's a hypothetical example: Imagine that a young person named Riley moves to a new town during high school. Riley is shy, sits in the back of classrooms at school and is afraid of speaking to new classmates. At the end of the first week of school, another student approaches Riley and asks if they want to join a Spanish study group that's preparing for the upcoming test. When Riley joins the study group and feels a sense of belonging, he feels more grounded in his new home, and these become Riley's closest friends until graduation. The other study group members, in turn, make some evaluations of Riley—they notice that the drawings that Riley makes while doodling in class are really elaborate. They tell Riley that he's good at art. Over time, these comments help Riley construct an identity as an artist, and Riley eventually goes to art school after graduation.

This story shows the way that various members of our community often have a profound impact on our sense of self and the story we construct about ourselves over time. This also means that other people have tremendous power to both impact our identity or sense of self for good and for ill. For instance, when someone experiences an interpersonal trauma, their story is impacted negatively by the person who harmed them. One form this takes is that the victimized party may feel that the perpetrating party impacted their story in a way they did not consent to. This was the case with Chanel Miller, the woman who was sexually violated by Stanford student Brock Turner while unconscious. Miller writes in her memoir that while she was in the hospital, she was asked to sign a set of documents, and in that moment, she began to recognize that Turner had played a role in her story that she did not consent to:

> A stack of papers were set in front of me. My arm snaked out of the blankets to sign. If they explained what I was consenting to, it was lost on me. Papers and papers, all different colors, light purple, yellow, tangerine. No one explained why my underwear was gone, why my hands were bleeding, why my hair was dirty, why I was dressed in funny pants, but things seemed to be moving right along, and I figured if I kept signing and nodding, I would come out of this place cleaned up and set right again. I put my name at the bottom, a big loop *C* and two lumps for the *M*. I stopped when I saw the words **Rape Victim** in bold at the top of one sheet. A fish leapt out of the water. I paused. No, I do not consent to being a rape victim. If I signed on the line, would I become one? If I refused to sign, could I remain my regular self?[8]

What Miller's reflection on that moment illustrates is the way that a trauma is not only violating because of the concrete details of what happened but because of its narrative element. In Miller's case, she neither consented to the rape itself nor to her new status as "victim." In other words, she didn't consent to the role that Brock Turner cast her into because of his actions.

In cases of interpersonal trauma, the narrative violation doesn't just emerge from the absence of consent. It also occurs because victimized parties are unable to enact agency over the narrative of their lives. In non-traumas, individuals can often exert some degree of narrative agency—they can decide what to eat, who to talk to, whether to cut their hair. The enactment of agency isn't always effective, but to some extent, each of us is able to act and have our actions understood. Indeed, this enactment of agency or the attempt to meet our desires is part of what makes us human.[9] In trauma, however, that narrative agency gets challenged or even temporarily eradicated by the harm. As a result, the victimized party's story doesn't just stop. It also becomes unclear whether that person can or will be able to continue to write the story at all.

As a result of trauma's narrative effects, it can often seem as if the result is a shattered sense of self. No longer does the self seem to have a story that flows and develops over the course of time. The story has stopped and along with that closure, assumptions about who the victimized party was and what their place in the world was no longer seem to make sense. A person may no longer feel safe if they experience trauma at the hands of someone they love, and they may question their ability to effectively evaluate the character of others. If they blame themselves for the trauma, they may judge themselves negatively, think they're responsible for the harm, or they may attribute global character deficits to themselves, such as thinking they're "evil" or "tarnished" or "bad." Trauma survivors, therefore, not only experience trauma as a stalled story. They also experience it as a story in which their character is no longer who it seemed to be.

The narrative foreclosure that trauma brings about also affects a person's sense of time, because time seems to have stopped along with the story of their lives. This is a peculiar quirk of trauma: Because of the way trauma works in the brain, it causes individuals to feel stuck in time. Meanwhile, the world seems to be moving on without them—other people seem to be able to experience joy, to enact agency, to move forward in their narrative journey. But for the traumatized person, the trauma seems to color everything in their lives so that their world—and time with it—seem to stop. In other words, traumatized individuals often feel trapped in the event itself, and so it becomes difficult for them to feel as if their story can be reconstructed. Likewise, it may become hard to see how their sense of self or the narrative of their lives could be reconstructed beyond its shattered state. As a result, words like "hope" or "dream" or "imagine" or "future" no longer seem to apply because the trauma seems to have broken a person's sense of self and stopped the story in its tracks, robbing the person of the trust or agency needed to move it forward.[10]

Trauma as Spiritual

Individuals may encounter profound spiritual consequences from living through a trauma. As pastoral theologian Carrie Doehring observes, many who encounter trauma simultaneously encounter challenges posed to their **embedded beliefs**, or core beliefs, practices, and values that tended to be unexamined and instilled during the course of childhood.[11] Some may lose their faith in that battle, as their embedded beliefs about a "good God" clash with the horror of the trauma. The grief and confusion that result from a loss of faith can be profoundly destabilizing. Moreover, some may maintain a belief in God but feel that the God they believed in is not the same. They may likewise feel that any assumptions they had about God's plan for them have been thrown out the window, replaced with a certain degree of chaos and uncertainty. There is no longer a meta-narrative, no longer a destiny or a purpose to one's life or the universe. Or, if there is a purpose, it doesn't seem to be a very life-giving one.[12]

Some people may try to reconcile the logical disjunct they face by asking questions related to theodicy, such as, "Why did this bad thing happen to me?" Sometimes, individuals will answer these questions negatively, concluding that God does not love them or has abandoned them. They may even believe that God has done so because they deserved to be punished or because they have a shameful character. Researchers have found that such negative religious coping strategies often emerge when individuals believe in an authoritarian God. In contrast, when individuals believe in a loving God, then faith tends to function as a positive religious coping strategy in the aftermath of an event like a trauma.[13] Spiritual caregivers, therefore, must be aware that many factors beyond the pragmatics of the trauma influence how a person responds to it spiritually. I will say more about this in chapters 2, 3, and 4.

The Dimensions of Trauma Transmission

One way to think of trauma's transmission is to think of it in terms of horizontal and vertical dimensions. Horizontally, trauma often transmits across a community, originating with the victim(s) and extending outward to their friends, family, and the wider community. In other words, the horizontal transmission of trauma is much like the bands of impact after an earthquake. One of the insidious parts of these bands is that much like an earthquake's Richter scale measurements, the impact may appear to be less as the trauma gets more and more distant from its locus; however, the distance from a traumatic event doesn't necessarily measure its effect on a given person's life, much like the number on a Richter scale may not directly correlate to damage done by an earthquake. A person may be more or less susceptible to trauma due to a number of factors including their prior experience of trauma, their biochemistry, and their social support system. Likewise, if a person is living in a building that is more susceptible to earthquakes, they may experience more damage than someone whose house was closer to the center but designed to withstand the force.

As a spiritual caregiver, it is important to be aware of how trauma transmits horizontally for several reasons. First, many people assume that trauma only affects the person who directly experienced it, and they may not be aware that trauma can affect people who were *vicariously* involved in the event. Such forms of trauma are known as **secondary trauma**. Victims of secondary trauma may have complicated feelings about the trauma precisely because they do not feel they ought to be affected as deeply as they are. One way that spiritual caregivers can help is by explaining that secondary trauma is real, as acknowledging it both gives a name to the experience and lessens any stigma or shame.

In addition to the way that trauma transmits horizontally, it also transmits vertically across generations. For instance, imagine a couple who has three children. The middle child dies at a young age due to cancer. As a result, the whole family is traumatized. The remaining children in the family grow up with the story and, in the case of the oldest, the memory of their deceased sibling. When the remaining two children are adults, they become anxious parents because they carry the trauma of their youth with them; they worry about their own children and are afraid they might die during childhood. At times, they're unaware that their fears are unconsciously related to the death of their sibling. Their own children may never have heard of the relative that died, but they do sense the anxiety, fear, and worry that pervades their households, and it affects them as a result.

This example shows how **intergenerational trauma** may occur within a family system over generations, but it can also occur collectively as a society over generations. For instance, studies have shown that the descendants of Holocaust survivors and slaves may experience intergenerational trauma because of how their ancestors were traumatized due to their identity. Likewise, Peter Loewenberg describes how he learned that his parents lived through a period of severe malnourishment in Germany during World War I that occurred due to a British blockade. This prolonged hunger crisis led to 750,000 deaths, a decline in births, as well as a decline in birth weight. The lack of nourishment was so profound that it led to permanent, stunted growth among the generation of children growing up in Germany at the time. Loewenberg suggests that this hunger trauma filtered down through a generation to those who were alive during the Nazi ascendence that led to World War II, encompassing the children who the Nazis attempted to convert to their beliefs. Indeed, he wonders whether those Germans were more susceptible to Nazi propaganda because of "how much of the concentration camp cruelty and hunger regimen was reversal and undoing, turning the passive experiences of childhood starvation into the active infliction of suffering on to innocent others three decades later."[14] Loewenberg further hypothesizes that the absence of parents during this period of deprivation may have made Hitler's charisma "attractive" to a generation of German children—now grown—who were looking for a parent figure who would return suddenly to protect the family. Indeed, this was a trope that gained prominence in Germany during the period between the end of World War I and the beginning of World War II.[15]

For some communities who grapple with collective intergenerational trauma, the trauma is simultaneously in the past and ongoing. Consider, for instance, the trauma experienced by Indigenous people in the United States. History tells us that white settlers in the United States robbed Indigenous people of their lands, forcibly relocating them onto land that wasn't historically theirs and that was often difficult to farm. Many suffered and died on the Trail of Tears or through the trauma of boarding schools that were established to shame Indigenous children into disavowing their cultural heritage in order to adopt Western language and beliefs, often exposing them to physical, emotional, and sexual abuse in the process. While these events remain in the past, the trauma of the collective subjugation of Indigenous people in the United States continues to take new forms. Case in point: In the 2022 case known as *Oklahoma v. Castro-Huerta*, the Supreme Court undid decades of legal precedent and simultaneously reduced the power of Indigenous tribes when it ruled that they did not have the right to prosecute non-Indigenous individuals who committed crimes on their land. Such cases, they ruled, needed to be referred to the state or federal government because, according to Brett Kavanaugh, who wrote the majority opinion, "Indian country within a state's territory is part of a state, not separate from a state."[16] Such a ruling indicates that tribal sovereignty is still under threat, as the rights of Indigenous people are once again taken away from them. The trauma that emerged from the evisceration of Indigenous sovereignty is therefore not a thing of the past but rather is historical intergenerational trauma *and* a trauma that continues in the present day.

People who experience intergenerational trauma may feel that they have been given the task of grappling with traumas they did not physically live through. To heal from such forms of trauma, one of the tasks that individuals face is finding ways to both integrate the traumatic past into the narrative of their lives while separating one's identity from it.[17] However, this can only be done when the trauma has ended, and in some cases, intergenerational, collective trauma is an ongoing event.

Trauma in Children

Children who experience trauma may present symptoms that are somewhat different than what we see in adults, but the reality of childhood trauma is no less ubiquitous. The US Department of Health and Human Services reports that two-thirds of children will have experienced at least one potentially traumatic event by age sixteen.[18] The CDC reports that one in five high school students experience school violence every year,[19] and one in seven will experience abuse or neglect.[20]

Children who experience trauma may struggle with attachment, especially if a caregiver was responsible for the harm. Most young children, for instance, will prefer to return to a home where abuse occurs than be moved to a safe environment because of the strong attachment they have to caregivers, even if the caregivers hurt them.[21] As a result, children may grow up with forms of **insecure attachment**. For instance, they may have a specific type of **attachment style** called an **anxious attachment** style in which they have difficulty trusting others and thereby have trouble developing close relationships. Alternatively, they may have an **avoidant attachment** style in which they tend to disconnect or be unable to develop emotional intimacy with others. Or, finally, they may have an anxious-avoidant or **disorganized attachment** style in which both tendencies present themselves, such that someone may initially attempt to trust others but then back off as soon as that relationship seems like it's getting too intense.

In addition, children who experience trauma may have difficulty developing a clear sense of self or healthy self-esteem. Case in point:

A child whose caregivers repeatedly tell them that they're adorable and clever will come to believe they are adorable and clever. As a result, if this child encounters abuse or harm later in life, they may be more able to identify it as such and respond with outrage or a sense of injustice because they have a healthy sense of self. Alternatively, when caregivers abuse or neglect a child, the child's initial experiences of themselves come to be rooted in shame or disgust, so if that child encounters further abuse down the line, they may be more apt to believe they deserve the harm because it aligns with the initial assessment they made of themselves as "bad."[22]

Finally, race can play a role in whether trauma is recognized in children or not. One study found that implicit bias on the part of counselors may cause them to diagnose Black and Latinx youth with conduct disorder (CD) or oppositional defiant disorder (ODD) rather than post-traumatic stress disorder, even when children meet the criteria for PTSD.[23] Not only is that problematic for treatment, but it also makes it, unfortunately, more likely that others might label the child as "poorly behaved" or "bad" because of the way that ODD and CD can be perceived as global deficits in character. It therefore becomes important for spiritual caregivers to recognize that they too may have such a bias which may make them more likely to label a child from a non-white background as "poorly behaved" rather than "traumatized."

Trauma versus PTSD

If the defining characteristic of a trauma is distress, then the defining characteristic of PTSD is distress *over time*. In other words, a trauma is highly distressing in the short-term, but if that distress persists for more than one month, then an individual may have PTSD. Approximately 30 percent of individuals who are exposed to a traumatic stressor develop PTSD, meaning that a majority of people who experience a trauma do not go on to develop the disorder. Anyone can develop PTSD, regardless of age, and approximately 7.8 percent of people in the United States will develop the condition over the course of a lifetime.[24] Of those, more than half are women.[25] The condition can occur both in those who directly lived through a trauma as well as in those who experienced secondary trauma, meaning they lived through the event vicariously.

A number of factors—including prior exposure to trauma and lack of social support—increase the likelihood that someone will develop PTSD, which can cause severe impairment in a person's ability to function in their life, including in their job and social relationships.[26] Symptoms often appear shortly after the trauma, but they may also have a latency period, meaning they do not appear for months or years. Individuals with PTSD are also apt to develop depression, anxiety, or substance abuse disorders concurrently. It is worth noting that researchers are increasingly aware the symptoms may present differently at different ages and within different cultures. In particular, researchers have found that the physiological symptoms tend to be more universal than the behavioral or mood-based ones are, perhaps because these are likely to have been impacted by the way cultural norms intersect with socialization.[27]

PTSD symptoms can be clustered into four categories. First, there are **intrusive symptoms**. These include:

1. Recurring memories of the event
2. Nightmares related to the event
3. Severe emotional or physiological distress that occurs upon being reminded of the event
4. Conscious or unconscious reenactments of the event
5. Recurring visits to the site of the event
6. Flashbacks, or a sense that one is physically and emotionally reliving the event

Intrusive symptoms make the individual hyperaware that the event occurred. One reason this may happen is because the brain is trying to keep the event in the forefront of thought as a protective measure—if a person does not forget the event, then perhaps their guard will be up enough to keep it from happening again.

In contrast to the intrusion symptoms, individuals with PTSD also experience **avoidance symptoms**. Such symptoms include:

1. Emotional numbing
2. Avoidance of activities, people, or places that reminisce the trauma
3. Attempts to avoid talking, thinking about, or remembering the trauma

These symptoms can function as a form of denial because if a person doesn't have to be reminded of the trauma, then they won't have to deal with the uncomfortable emotions or existential questions that accompany it. These symptoms may also serve a protective role, at least initially, because if the trauma makes a person unsafe, then that isn't the time to acknowledge or process the trauma. Indeed, the lack of safety may make direct acknowledgment too risky. An example of this might be a child who experiences abuse—they may use avoidance symptoms to cope during the trauma and in its immediate aftermath. These avoidance symptoms may initially serve a protective role and help the child survive the terrible reality that their caregivers fell down on the job. However, the child may also continue to experience avoidance symptoms for quite some time after the trauma ends because the symptoms have become part of their way of being in the world. At this stage, avoidance symptoms may be getting in the way, as they may be keeping the child (now an adult) from processing the trauma and forming healthy relationships with others.

It is helpful to recognize that individuals can vacillate between intrusive and avoidance symptoms, even in short periods of time. Mental health professionals refer to this phenomenon as the "dialectic of trauma."[28] This occurs because people instinctually alternate between a desire to name the trauma and to deny it, or, put differently, they struggle with wanting to recognize the horror and to avoid the reality that such horrors can occur in their world.

In addition, it may seem as if these two clusters of symptoms—avoidance and intrusive symptoms—don't belong together because they appear to be in opposition to one another. In other words, it may not seem to make sense that someone with PTSD simultaneously seems to be so aware of the trauma while also avoiding it. This disjunct may become particularly relevant in situations where traumas result in criminal proceedings in which a victim is called to the stand and asked to testify about their experiences. Because trauma survivors often have a heightened memory of some parts of the trauma (an intrusive symptom) while at the same time have forgotten other aspects of it (an avoidance symptom), lawyers may suggest that they have a faulty memory and discredit their claims. The assumption the lawyers make is that reliable memory is the same as complete memory. In other words, if some parts of the memory have been forgotten, then one can extrapolate that the remaining parts may be damaged, or that exonerating evidence may be omitted. The trouble with this way of interpreting survivor memory is that it fails to recognize that such gaps aren't necessarily evidence that a trauma didn't occur; they could just as easily be evidence that a trauma *did* occur.

Adding to the intrusive and avoidance symptoms mentioned above, there are two other clusters of symptoms that are part of the current PTSD diagnosis. One involves negative changes to thought or mood. Symptoms of this change include:

1. A sense of detachment from loved ones
2. Loss of interest in previously enjoyed activities
3. Hopelessness in regard to the future
4. Problems remembering parts of the trauma
5. Difficulty feeling positive emotions
6. Negative thoughts about oneself or the world in general
7. Difficulty making or keeping close relationships

Many of the symptoms above appear similar to those that are present in major depression. One difference between major depression and PTSD, however, is the cause. PTSD is the only diagnosis in the ***DSM*** (the manual used by mental health professionals to make diagnoses) that has a concrete origin. This is also referred to as an **etiological event**. In other words, PTSD emerges from a root cause, namely, the event that the person or community experienced as a trauma. In major depression, an etiological event is not necessary for a diagnosis. (It is worth noting that many individuals with PTSD also receive a major depression diagnosis.)

Finally, individuals with PTSD often experience a change in their arousal reactions, also known as their physiological and emotional reactions. Symptoms in this category include:

1. Difficulty sleeping or concentrating
2. Irrational outbursts of anger or aggression
3. Heightened startle or fear response
4. Feelings of shame and guilt
5. Self-destructive acts

It is important to be aware that these symptoms may not appear directly in relationship to the trauma and may wind up being projected onto others, including spiritual caregivers. Because spiritual caregivers are often perceived as being "safe" individuals, they are likely to be individuals who encounter the difficult emotions that people discharge in the wake of a trauma, whether or not they're directly related to it. In other words, the difficult emotions that individuals experience can be projected onto the caregiver. For example, a parishioner with PTSD may become irrationally angry because the liturgy has changed. The change isn't a major one, and when it was discussed at a meeting of the liturgy committee, everyone thought it was a good idea. However, when the rector announces it to the congregation, the parishioner with PTSD seems incensed, leaving the rector with the feeling that the anger is out of proportion to the change. The rector also has a nagging sense that something else is behind it.

Children and PTSD

The symptoms discussed above are the ones most commonly seen in adults who suffer from the PTSD, but children can also experience the disorder. The symptoms of older children and teens may resemble the symptoms seen in adults; this age group may also engage in disruptive or destructive acts or want to seek revenge for wrongs done to them. In young children, symptoms may involve:

1. Struggling to, or forgetting how, to talk
2. Wetting the bed
3. Becoming clingy with a caregiver
4. Reenacting the event in play

In both children and adults, PTSD is a disorder that requires support beyond what a spiritual care professional can offer. It is important that individuals who are presenting symptoms of PTSD seek out support from mental health professionals who are trained to deal with the condition, as a number of effective therapeutic interventions and medications are available to treat it. While spiritual care providers aren't equipped to offer this kind of support, they can still be essential to helping those who are struggling with PTSD. Knowing what the symptoms of PTSD are, they can be on the lookout for them in the people they care for so that they can help them get the support they need. Additionally, by encouraging individuals to get therapy, spiritual care providers have an opportunity to show that mental health struggles aren't something to be embarrassed about or something that ought to be stigmatized. Rather, PTSD is a morally neutral condition that requires care for wellness to return, and by educating their communities about PTSD, spiritual care providers can help others to recognize symptoms and seek support for themselves and their loved ones.

Secondary Trauma and Caregiving

Secondary—or vicarious—trauma occurs when a person hears about someone else's trauma but does not directly experience it. It is also commonly known as "compassion fatigue." Secondary trauma can lead to symptoms like those seen in PTSD, including anxiety, isolation, sleep problems, hypervigilance, emotional exhaustion, confusion, and helplessness.[29] It is considered an occupational hazard for helping professionals—including spiritual caregivers—who work with traumatized populations. Left untreated, secondary trauma can cause cognitive, emotional, physical, and psychological distress. It may also contribute to someone leaving their profession for a different line of work in which exposure to hearing about trauma is less common.

There are some ways that spiritual caregivers can support themselves prior to and during an episode of secondary trauma. First, it's important that they understand the symptoms of secondary trauma and have a robust support network that they can call upon for help. As in first-hand trauma, connections matter. Additionally, caregivers can support themselves by taking steps to prevent secondary trauma from occurring. These include maintaining robust wellness practices like taking time for relaxation, exercise, and the arts. Taking time to engage with the natural world through gardening or hiking may also promote a sense of groundedness or wellness. Caregivers also need to make sure their own needs are met and that they're practicing a healthy work-life balance that includes appropriate time off. Finally, caregivers can prevent secondary trauma by looking at how the organizations they work for engage with trauma, because organizations can experience secondary trauma, just as individuals can. Secondary trauma within an organization can impact the extent to which it functions effectively and the extent to which it can reasonably care for caregivers and prevent additional trauma from occurring.

Caregivers can buffer themselves against the effects of secondary trauma by regularly engaging in body-based grounding practices, including meditation, participation in liturgies, yoga, and deep breathing. Becoming fluent in competencies like **self-differentiation** and spiritual **self-reflexivity** can also help caregivers to practice in a healthy way that both meets the needs of care seekers while helping them to keep healthy boundaries so that their work with trauma-informed populations remains sustainable.[30]

A Way Forward

This chapter has illustrated how trauma is a complex phenomenon that affects the whole self of individuals who experience it. As a result, it takes an approach that responds to the whole self in order to alleviate distress. This approach often involves experts and community members from many walks of life. Medical and mental health experts have crucial resources that can help traumatized people experience physiological and psychological relief. These include different forms of therapy and medications that target the symptoms that a person might be experiencing. Traumatized individuals can also make use of other resources that promote healing and wellness, including the arts and yoga. Yoga has been shown by trauma expert Bessel van der Kolk to be an effective resource for trauma survivors because of the way that it promotes deep breathing, helps individuals feel grounded, and allows them to regain a sense of trust in their bodies.[31] Additionally, traumatized individuals often turn to the arts as a way to express complicated or strong emotions, including anger, sadness, frustration, helplessness, lament, shame, and remorse. For instance, Chanel Miller—the young woman described earlier in the chapter who was raped by Brock Turner—used several art forms to help her heal, including writing, printmaking, and drawing. Other survivors have turned to different art forms, including music or dance.

In addition to the arts, yoga, medical, and psychological sciences, the support of friends and family is often essential to survivors healing from trauma. However, many trauma survivors can feel as if they've lost the ability to trust within their communities. This can occur when the community itself is the source of the trauma. One high-profile example of this is the sex abuse scandal within the Roman Catholic Church. Many of the survivors of the abuse were harmed by clergy who represented the Church as an organization, and as a result, survivors turned away from the organization after the abuse because they felt that the Church did little to protect them or because they knew that a public accusation would cause them to be alienated from the congregation, who would side with the perpetrating priest and not with them. Some also felt that their faith in God was harmed, and so they did not want to return to their church, even though they'd been close with members of the community prior. Trauma, in other words, can cause individuals to lose the people they most valued. However, when communities function as a means of support, they can also be essential resources for survivor healing. This is because they can help restore trust, create a safe space for the survivor to share the story of the harm, and, in turn, help the survivor to begin to reconstruct their sense of self and see how the trauma fits into the narrative of their lives. Spiritual care providers can therefore be part of this community of support and can also play an essential role in healing from trauma because of their unique skills.

It is important to recognize that trauma takes many forms and often requires a multidisciplinary approach to heal. Effective spiritual care is but one component of that approach. It is essential that spiritual care providers understand that survivors often need therapeutic resources and other forms of support, and as a result, it becomes necessary for them to have resources to share with survivors. Some resources to have on hand include a list of therapists (especially ones that might take payment on a sliding scale), contact information for the local rape crisis center and domestic abuse shelter, and phone numbers for local social service agencies, including suicide and crisis hotlines. These resources, alongside spiritual care, can be essential for a trauma survivor to receive the support they need to heal their whole self and to move forward with the story of their lives.

CHAPTER TWO

Safety

Introduction

In 1997, the psychiatrist Judith Herman published what would become one of the most groundbreaking texts about the nature and treatment of trauma—a book called *Trauma and Recovery*. Herman recognized that trauma comes in many forms. Instead of assuming that it occurred only in isolated, rare instances—likely related to military combat—she asserted that trauma is a common part of human experience, and she proposed an assessment for its complex forms, as well as a three-stage treatment model. First, the traumatized person needs to rediscover a sense of safety. Second, they need an opportunity to process the trauma emotionally through meaning-making activities like remembrance and mourning. Third, they need to engage in acts that allow them to reconnect to their community as someone who has integrated the trauma into their lives.

While spiritual care providers are not trained to help individuals process traumas at a psychotherapeutic level, they can nonetheless engage in these three stages in targeted interventions that may help resolve the spiritual struggles that trauma initiates or exacerbates.[1] The following three chapters therefore explore each stage of Herman's recovery process and how spiritual care providers can provide support for each. This chapter will thus begin with safety, addressing what safety is from multiple perspectives before proceeding to consider how a lack of safety manifests in a person's spiritual life and what care providers can do to help.

What is Safety?

Safety is like the ozone layer. It protects, buffers, and it offers a kind of coverage that allows regular business to go on as usual. When humans have enough safety, they may not pay much attention to it, but without it, they realize the threat a that a lack of safety precipitates via exposure and vulnerability to physical, psychological, and spiritual harms. Humans thus need safety as much as the earth needs the ozone layer to provide a base level of protection in order for life to thrive. A lack of safety threatens human existence.

In this way, there is an observable and quantifiable quality to some forms of safety—a person either has clothes or they do not. They either have a home to live in, or they do not. They can either pay their utility bills, or they cannot. Other elements of safety, however, are less obvious, less concrete. They can be better described as a general feeling of protection. This **felt sense of safety** is also essential to our existence, keeping fear from dominating our lives and creating space for experiences like joy and trust. Like trauma, then, safety encompasses the whole self, which means that safety presents in multiple different ways. Spiritual caregivers benefit from an awareness of these so that they can both recognize the presence of safety as well as its absence. To that end, what follows is a discussion of three dimensions through which people experience safety—physical, psychological, and spiritual.

Physical Safety

Physical safety is the sense that one is safe in one's own body and is not actively being exposed to physical danger. Trauma survivors may be well-aware that physical safety is not guaranteed in life; indeed, they may have had experiences in which their physical safety was put at risk. Examples of compromised physical safety include experiencing an illness, being abused by another person, or having one's home or car vandalized. A first priority of any caregiver—spiritual or otherwise—is to ensure that physical safety needs are met to the best of their ability. Helping a survivor get proper medical attention, a safe place to live, and reliable transportation are some ways that a caregiver can help practically with the need for physical safety. It will therefore be helpful for caregivers to familiarize themselves with organizations in their local area that provide these resources so that they can call upon them easily when needed. If a caregiver is unsure of how to proceed, it may be helpful to ask others in their geographical area for help. Helpful contacts may include local religious leaders, social workers, school psychologists, medical professionals, and leaders in social service organizations.

Physical safety may also be compromised when an individual is a threat to themselves. Many traumatized individuals suffer so profoundly that they may engage in practices of self-harm—including addictive behaviors—or may consider or try to take their own life. It is important that caregivers become comfortable asking questions about whether a person is engaging in such behaviors, including becoming comfortable asking whether someone is considering suicide. In cases where a person's immediate physical safety is at risk—for instance, in a case where a person may be considering suicide—the caregiver should seek immediate support helping the person to procure the necessary resources for safety. One way to do this is to enlist friends and family to take the person to the local emergency room so they can receive a psychological evaluation.[2] In the United States, caregivers can also call the Suicide and Crisis Hotline (988) for assistance. Many areas also have a local crisis hotline that can send a professional to meet the individual who is struggling. It may also be necessary to call for an ambulance to take the person to an emergency room if they are a danger to themselves.[3] The caregiver should not leave the person alone during this time.

Finally, caregivers can help provide physical safety by making sure the physical environment in which they offer care is safe. There are several ways to ensure this safety. One is to avoid physically touching care seekers. Many individuals with a history of trauma can be triggered by touch. Touching anyone without permission can also violate their own sense of agency. In cases of spiritual caregiving, the avoidance of touch is particularly important because the caregiver is in a position of power relative to the care seeker, both due to their professional identity and because they aren't rendering themselves vulnerable through disclosing harm. Moreover, physical touch can be confusing to a care seeker, in part because it challenges the boundaries of a professional relationship. Inappropriate touch can therefore not only be triggering but also a violation of the caregiver's power.

Some caregivers may respond that avoiding an asexual form of touch—for instance, a hug—can make the caregiver seem cold or the conversation impersonal. Underlying this concern is an assumption that touch signals empathy and understanding, and sometimes, it is true that it does. However, there are other ways to practice empathy and understanding that do not require touch, and, indeed, many of these are best practices in spiritual caregiving. Examples of such practices include active listening, asking open-ended questions, restating what the care seeker just said in the conversation, and so forth. These practices are preferable to physical touch because they do not run the risk of physical violation.

Avoiding physical touch is not the only way that a caregiver can help create an environment of physical safety for the care seeker. In addition, they may engage in physically grounding practices that the care seeker finds meaningful. These might include a body scan, centering prayer, or silent meditation. The caregiver can ask the care seeker's input as to what kind of grounding exercise they would find meaningful as a way of helping the care seeker to restore agency.

Additionally, caregivers can take steps to ensure that the space in which they offer care is private without being secretive.[4] A private environment ensures reasonable confidentiality while a secretive environment allows for the abuse of power, which is the antithesis of what caregivers seek to provide. There are several ways to provide physical safety in the caregiving space that meet this criterion. For instance, caregivers can meet with care seekers in public locations. These may be indoors or outdoors, as long as they aren't isolated. The benefit of a public setting is that the presence of other people adds an additional layer of protection, a kind of check or balance against the possibility that the caregiver could exploit their power unnoticed.

If a public location is not a possibility, caregivers can take steps to enhance the safety of their offices. For instance, they can do their best to avoid meeting the care seeker when they are alone in their workplace setting. They can also make sure that the door has a window, or, alternatively, leave the door ajar. Both options ensure that the caregiver cannot abuse power without being noticed by others in the building. If the door is left ajar and the care seeker is concerned that what they say may be overheard, a white noise machine can be used. Keeping the door ajar or having a window in one's door helps keep the space open and transparent and becomes a check and balance against wrongdoing. Additionally, caregivers can try to avoid placing any barriers between the place where a care seeker sits and the office door. Especially for care seekers with a history of trauma, it can be helpful for them to know that there is an exit nearby, should they feel overwhelmed or unsafe during the conversation. Finally, caregivers will benefit from making any place where they schedule a meeting as physically accessible as possible. This signals to care seekers that all are welcome in the space, regardless of their physical abilities. It also makes it easier for an individual to seek out a conversation if they know that they can access the space.

Psychological Safety

Trauma survivors will likely reexperience symptoms as they explore memories and the meanings of those memories in a spiritual care setting. It is therefore important for care seekers to have helpful ways of coping during these times. Body-based spiritual self-care becomes an essential coping mechanism in this regard, and it will be important for these practices to become part of the care seeker's routine. Such practices include—but are not limited to—centering prayer, yoga, deep breathing, and walking outside. They can also become the core of the survivor's psychological sense of safety.

Psychologically, a person experiences safety when they feel trusted within a group or when they are able to express themselves freely.[5] Experts who study psychological safety understand it to be group-based, meaning that it takes more than just a feeling within oneself or a relationship with one other person to feel psychologically safe. Instead, psychological safety emerges from the overall culture of the group of which one is a part. If conditions within that group cause a person to feel respected or allow them to feel that they can speak their mind without retribution, then the conditions facilitate psychological safety. Psychological safety also helps people take risks because if they feel safe within a group, then they may be more likely to be able to say something or do something that feels authentic or vulnerable to them. Understandably, people are more likely to take self-protective measures without this kind of psychological safety.

In cases where individuals do not feel psychologically safe, they may experience a phenomenon known as **emotional flooding**. Emotional flooding involves a feeling that one is being overwhelmed by strong, uncontrollable feelings. When a person is in a state of emotional flooding, their limbic system is in overdrive, making it hard to engage in activities that involve logic or planning. Indeed, it may be next to impossible to have a constructive or in-depth conversation with someone who is experiencing a period of emotional flooding. In addition to emotional flooding, trauma survivors often experience other disconcerting symptoms, like dissociation and disengagement, that may also cause them to feel a sense that they are not safe or grounded. To help alleviate these symptoms, it may be helpful for care seekers to engage in body-based spiritual self-care, which can help restore a sense of safety and can also help care seekers develop self-compassion. Caregivers can help by recommending such activities and by engaging in physically grounding activities to help restore a sense of stability to the care seeker. If the caregiver is unable to help with the strategies they have at their disposal, it may be necessary to contact a crisis hotline service, the person's therapist, or local emergency services.

Finally, caregivers can provide psychological safety by ensuring **reasonable confidentiality**. This element of psychological safety has two parts: *confidentiality* and *reasonableness*. Confidentiality, broadly speaking, means that caregivers will not repeat what a care seeker says during a caregiving conversation. Care seekers benefit from knowing that what they say will usually remain confidential because it communicates the boundaries of the caregiving relationship. It also signals that the caregiver has narrative respect for the care seeker. It is, after all, the care seeker's story that is being disclosed, and that story is also theirs to share or repeat. When care seekers know that confidentiality will be maintained, it also allows them to speak more freely, knowing that the caregiver will not be sharing what is said outside of the conversation. In cases where the caregiver and care seeker have many mutual acquaintances—say, in a parish context—it also helps the care seeker to know that what they share will not become the stuff of gossip. Confidentiality can therefore provide a sense of psychological safety for the care seeker.

Not all conversations, however, can ethically be kept confidential. This is where the element of *reasonableness* comes in. This term limits confidentiality, signaling that there are times when sharing what has been confided is ultimately the right thing to do. Breaking confidentiality can occur for several reasons, all of which ultimately should be in the interest of protecting the care seeker. For instance, the best practice of spiritual care providers is to break confidentiality in cases where the care seeker plans to hurt themselves or others. Ethically, this is the right thing to do, both to protect the care seeker and the wider community. In addition, laws often limit confidentiality o protect those who are vulnerable.[6] To that end, many states in the United States impose limits on confidentiality in matters of child abuse, elder abuse, or in cases where the person being abused is disabled. Usually, spiritual caregivers are subject to these limits, and as a result, the caregiver is usually required to disclose claims of abuse and neglect to legal authorities within a certain period (i.e. within twenty-hours after the disclosure). Someone who is required to report such abuse to the government is known as a **mandated reporter**. Those in helping professions—such as teachers, doctors, and therapists—are often included in mandated reporting laws. Spiritual care providers should become familiar with the mandated reporting laws where they live, as these vary by state.

In addition to legal limits on confidentiality, many organizations also expressly limit what can be kept confidential for the sake of the care seeker. For instance, some college campuses may require that employees disclose claims of sexual abuse or harassment to the school's Title IX Office if a student makes a complaint, which is responsible for responding to allegations of discrimination on the basis of sex. Additionally, many religious organizations require caregivers to notify government authorities or leaders in the organization if care seekers claim that abuse of a minor, disabled person, or elderly person occurred.

A person who discloses harm may feel a loss of psychological safety if they discover after the disclosure that it cannot be kept confidential. Indeed, they may feel anger or believe that the caregiver has misled them or is not trustworthy. One way to avoid this is to alert the care seeker as to the limits of confidentiality at the start of the conversation, prior to any disclosure. In that moment, the caregiver can also explain that these limits exist to protect those who are vulnerable. Such a statement may look like this: "Before we start, I want to let you know that I do my best to keep conversations confidential. However, there are some conversations that I can't do that with because it may lead to greater harm. So, I want to be transparent that I do have to share any reports of child abuse, elder abuse, or abuse of a disabled person to social services. I may also have to share what you tell me if you plan to hurt yourself or others. Do you have any questions that I can answer about that?"

Alerting individual care seekers as to the limits of confidentiality is not the only way that caregivers can make this boundary known. Another thing caregivers can do is to make sure this information is widely known throughout the organization where they work so that care seekers are familiar with these limits before they even come in for a conversation. This is most easily done in organizations where the caregiver has ongoing relationships with care seekers. If a caregiver does work in such a setting, widely disseminating the limits to confidentiality may prevent a sense of violation on the part of the care seeker during a disclosure and help them recognize that these limits are not a personal affront so much as an attempt to ensure the safety of the most vulnerable.

There are a number of ways that caregivers can teach their communities about the limits of confidentiality. They might, for instance, hold an educational forum or include the information in a sermon. They could also post a sign on their office that states the limits of confidentiality or routinely include it on newsletters from their organization. These are but a few ways to make this information more publicly known.

Publicly addressing confidentiality and its limits helps caregivers to establish healthy boundaries and also creates transparency between them and care seekers. Put differently, if care seekers know the limits of what can be kept confidential in advance of a disclosure, then there is less of a possibility that someone will be offended or feel ashamed. Publicly addressing the limits of confidentiality is also an educational opportunity. It acknowledges that abuse happens and that there are resources to help. It also holds the potential to destigmatize the victimized party because the caregiver can explain that abuse is never the victim's fault. This can help care seekers who may feel shame, embarrassment, or responsibility for the harm inflicted upon them. As a result, both the upholding of confidentiality and the acknowledgment of its limits provide opportunities for cultivating psychological safety in care seekers.

Spiritual Safety

Every human being has a unique relationship to spirituality that encompasses different beliefs, values, practices, and experiences. Some people experience organized religion and their spirituality as deeply intertwined. For those individuals, their beliefs and practices emerge directly from an organized religion's tenets, and they filter their experiences through it. For others, spirituality revolves around their relationship with a named divine being—often referred to as "God"—and they have only a loose affiliation with organized religion. Perhaps they were raised in an organized religion but no longer attend services, or perhaps their beliefs happen to align with a faith tradition, even though they do not see themselves as part of it. For still others, however, spirituality may primarily be more about a belief that there is something that transcends the self or a general sense that life is sacred. They may or may not have an affiliation with organized religion. People who do have such an affiliation include an increasing number of Americans who they say that they're "spiritual but not religious."[7] The spiritual but not religious group—also referred to as the "Nones"—may profoundly engage in spiritual experiences but may also be skeptical enough of organized religion that their beliefs and practices are not developed through formal participation in them.

When a person is spiritually safe, they feel comfortable exploring and expressing their beliefs, values, practices, and experiences—all aspects of what psychologists call their moral and spiritual orienting systems. A person who is spiritually safe, in other words, can be part of any religious tradition or none; they may believe in God or they may not. This is because spiritual safety does not revolve only around what a person believes but rather around many interacting aspects of their spiritual orienting systems, like their values, practices, experiences, and communities. That groundedness encompasses both the safety to be confident in one's beliefs *and* the safety to question them.

One reason a person may not feel spiritually safe is because aspects of their spirituality (or their spiritual orienting system) have not helped them cope positively in the aftermath of trauma. Relatedly, a person may feel spiritually unsafe if they know that their religious community is not safe or if religious authorities in their tradition are not trustworthy. In other words, these authorities and communities can also impact a person's ability to cope after a trauma. To that end, psychologists like Ken Pargament have found that values, beliefs, spiritual practices, and religious communities influence whether a person has positive or negative coping strategies. For instance, Pargament found that individuals tend to cope with life events better when they believe in a God who is loving and relational rather than one that is punitive and punishing.[8] He also found that those who are part of more authoritarian religious organizations tend to have more negative religious coping strategies.[9] These predictors have been found to impact health outcomes as well, with the former resulting in better outcomes than the latter.[10]

In terms of spiritual safety, one might extrapolate from Pargament's data that individuals feel less spiritually safe when they experience God as punitive. The love of this God, after all, can be taken away, sometimes for fickle or unclear reasons. Moreover, authoritarian religious organizations may be more apt to engage in and get away with religious abuse because of the lack of checks and balances within the organization and the inability of members to question beliefs or practices. For one example of what that might look like, consider a religious organization known as the FLDS. The FLDS—short for the **Fundamentalist Church of Jesus Christ of Latter-Day Saints**—is a religious group of fundamentalist **Mormons** who live on compounds without modern day technology and practice polygamy. Women in the group must adhere to a strict, conservative dress code and are told who to marry by the head of the organization (also known as the "Prophet"). Few attain higher education, and access to the outside world is severely curtailed. The Southern Poverty Law Center has labeled the FLDS a hate group because of its homophobic, racist, and sexist ideology and practices.[11] Often, the organization is referred to as a "cult" because members aren't allowed to have relationships—romantic or otherwise—with those outside of the organization, including relatives. Doing so, according to the FLDS, will threaten the likelihood that members will go to heaven.

The FLDS has been the source of multiple traumas for its members. Leaders routinely send boys away from the compound if they question the organization. Their lack of education and exposure to the outside world often leaves these "lost boys," as they've become known, without any way to provide for their basic needs. Meanwhile, leaders simultaneously force girls and women into polygamous marriages—which can be changed at the will of the leader—against their will and often while they're underage. It is perhaps unsurprising, therefore, that current and former members are apt to feel spiritually unsafe within the organization. Because of its authoritarian structure, there is little freedom and many opportunities for abuse to occur. Those who leave the organization experience isolation because they are unable to stay in contact with their family and friends within. Those who remain find they're unable to speak freely or voice critiques of the organization because the "Prophet," who is tantamount to God, is considered to be infallible and criticisms are not tolerated.[12] Such practices result in spiritual suffering for members, who are left confused, questioning their beliefs, without a community, and worried about the threats posed to their soul. Moreover, leaders of the organization use theology to exercise their power when they tell young girls that it is God's will for them to marry at a young age or terminate their marriage to one person and direct them to marry another. This kind of spiritual subjugation has spiritual consequences, as members have reported feeling confusion, fear that God is punishing them, or a desire to end their relationship with organized religion altogether in the aftermath of the abuse.

The dramatic example of the FLDS illustrates what the violation of spiritual safety looks like. Conversely, however, spirituality can also help individuals cope in times of trauma and in trauma's aftermath. Consider the story of Elizabeth Smart for but one illustration. At the age of fourteen, a man snuck into Smart's bedroom and abducted her. He then brought her to a secluded area where his wife was and, inspired by polygamous practices like those in the FLDS, performed a ritual which he stated turned her into his second wife. Smart spent nine months in captivity and was subjected to horrendous physical, psychological, sexual, and spiritual abuse. However, Smart was also a young woman with a deep faith, having been raised in a Mormon family (note that **The Church of Jesus Christ of Latter-Day Saints** is different from the FLDS). The belief system she inherited from the Mormon tradition and her parents described God as loving and sustaining; indeed, she didn't think it was possible for God to abandon her. Smart drew upon her faith daily during her abduction and eventually used her knowledge of it to convince her abductor to bring her back to Utah, where she believed it was more likely that someone would recognize and rescue her. To persuade him, she stated that she'd received a message from God instructing them to return to Salt Lake City, the headquarters of the Mormon faith.

Smart has publicly affirmed how her belief in a good and loving God sustained her during a period in which her abductor and his wife tried to convince her that she had no value, oftentimes using religious rhetoric to do so.[13] Her story is thus both one that illustrates what it looks like when someone tries to inflict spiritual trauma as much as it is a story of how someone used positive spiritual coping mechanisms to survive.

Examples like the ones above illustrate how important religious coping mechanisms can be. They can both help and harm care seekers. It can therefore be helpful for spiritual caregivers to help care seekers identify what their spiritual beliefs are and whether they function as positive or negative coping mechanisms. If their beliefs are currently functioning negatively, it may be helpful for caregivers to help raise awareness in care seekers about how those beliefs are operating in their lives and to present alternatives that might offer a more robust sense of spiritual safety.

On Isolation and Belief

The aftermath of trauma can often cause people to experience profound isolation. Sometimes, this isolation occurs because they feel that nobody will understand the depth of the difficulty that they're experiencing or that societal norms keep them from discussing such tender topics with others. In addition, some trauma survivors may feel there is so much stigma around their experiences that they do not want to make themselves vulnerable by talking about them. One example of when this might occur is in sexual violations.[14] As Kristen Leslie acknowledges, victims of sexual violations face barriers to being believed by others, including the idea that victims lie about the harm or that they were to blame somehow, perhaps by dressing provocatively, by consuming alcohol, or by being sexually promiscuous in the past.[15] Victimized individuals are usually well aware of how the people they care about, or the wider culture, have received other accusations in the past, and, in turn, they may be wary of making one themselves. They may feel that no good will come of speaking the truth if no one believes them and that they may be further harmed in the process.

The experience of not being believed or of not feeling that one can speak for fear of the consequences can lead to a profound sense of relational instability, or put differently, it may make people feel physically, psychologically, or spiritually unsafe in their relationships because they are aware that they cannot trust the people around them with the trauma. Spiritual caregivers can play an important role in healing by coming to conversations assuming belief. Often, they may be the only person who does. This may be because the victimized party is accusing someone who is beloved or has power in their community. It may be because the criminal justice system assumes innocence until a prosecutor proves guilt, thereby putting those who make accusations on the defensive. Or it may be because of stereotypes about people who make accusations, as in cases of sexual violations, where it is often assumed that the victimized party might want attention, "asked for" the harm due to how they dressed, or has something to gain by making the accusation.

Some survivors may also feel they cannot talk about the impact of the trauma because it brings up uncomfortable emotions like shame, grief, anger, and sadness. They may feel too vulnerable to share these feelings with another person, or they may feel that they do not want to hurt the people around them by sharing difficult aspects of the trauma. The discomfort that survivors may have with the feelings loved ones might show may extend from a desire to protect those they love, but the result is that the survivor winds up feeling a profound sense of isolation as a result. Such isolation can prevent them from getting the care they need for their own healing and cause the trauma to function as a barrier between them and the building of authentic relationships.

Another way that we can think of isolation is that it extends from a perceived lack of safety. Put differently, if an individual doesn't feel safe around members of their community, one way they can protect themselves is by limiting or cutting off those relationships. This protective measure, however, can backfire in the aftermath of trauma, because survivors need a supportive community for their own healing. One way that spiritual caregivers can help is by cultivating a different kind of relationship with the care seeker. By bringing the best practices of care to a conversation, they can model a relationship in which it is safe to talk about traumatic experiences, thereby helping to transcend the kinds of isolation that the person may have been feeling.

In cases where the spiritual caregiver is part of a larger faith community, caregivers can also assist by helping to mold the culture of that community into one where individuals can feel a sense of belonging and where all are welcomed, regardless of whether they have experienced trauma. One way that caregivers can do this is by educating their communities about trauma, including statistics about its prevalence and how it functions. They can also help others understand that victimized individuals have enough to struggle with without feeling stigmatized because of what they experienced, and that one way others can help is by welcoming the individual as a whole self, without prejudice or discrimination. In addition, caregivers may want to consider integrating grounding practices like centering prayer, meditation, and yoga into their regular rotation of offerings. Finally, they can help members of their community develop basic pastoral care skills, including active listening and the asking open-ended questions. Such practices can be used in their daily lives to enrich relationships across the board. Even if the person they're speaking with never discloses a trauma, utilizing some of these practices can help a care seeker feel a greater sense of safety and belonging because they know they're being listened to and respected by the listener.[16]

On Saying Too Much and Saying Too Little

The psychiatrist and trauma expert Bessel van der Kolk writes that he rarely asks his clients to disclose every detail of their traumatic past. Indeed, he never pushes clients to disclose because he knows that it's not necessarily relevant for treatment and, more importantly, it may be unhelpful to the client because it might push them into emotional territory that feels too overwhelming. Instead, he tries to create a safe environment for clients in which they can learn to "tolerate feeling what they feel and knowing what they know."[17] He refers to this practice as **Auden's Rule**, in reference to these lines from W. H. Auden's Poem, "New Year Letter":

> *Truth, like love and sleep, resents*
> *Approaches that are too intense.*[18]

Spiritual caregivers can learn quite a bit about cultivating safety from van der Kolk's approach. Their job is not to encourage the care seeker to disclose every aspect of the trauma as much as it is to create a safe space for them to say what feels comfortable in that moment. One way that spiritual caregivers can avoid going into the weeds about the trauma with care seekers is to remember the **gift of silence**. The gift of silence involves just what its name suggests—recognizing the value of silence and employing it as a gift in caregiving conversations. Such a practice is valuable for several reasons. First, when caregivers jump in as soon as the care seeker is done speaking, then it means that they were probably formulating their own thoughts during the care seeker's reflections. This means they weren't actively listening as closely as they could have been. Allowing some silence to enter the conversation means that the caregiver isn't simultaneously trying to listen and trying to figure out what to say at the same time, which means they can pay more attention to what the care seeker is saying. Silence also means the caregiver can be more intentional about crafting their own reply, which means the questions they ask can enrich the conversation more. In addition, silence creates space for the care seeker to discern whether they have more to say. Sometimes, the thing that's most weighing on their heart is the thing that gets spoken when given a little extra space. Finally, silence can instill groundedness in a conversation. It slows the pace of the conversation down, making it more intentional and less harried, which can be a welcome relief for anyone, especially a trauma survivor. It is also a very countercultural way of holding a conversation. Slowing down a conversation enough to create space for silence isn't something modeled very often, especially in the United States, which values productivity and the rat race mentality, so it can take some practice to do well.

Spiritual caregivers will also benefit from being intentional about *what* they say, in addition to valuing silence as a key component of conversations about trauma. Offering advice, for instance, is a problematic (if tempting) practice because it robs the care seeker of opportunities for their own discernment. It also robs them of narrative agency which—recalling the last chapter—was one of the parts of the self that gets damaged in the trauma. There are a few reasons that caregivers may be tempted to jump into advice mode. One is that they're uncomfortable with the difficult subject matter being covered in a conversation about trauma and consciously—or subconsciously—are seeking a way to avoid it. Another reason that caregivers offer advice is that they genuinely believe it will work due to their own experience with the event, either first-person or otherwise. The problem with this approach is that what works for one person may not work for another. Offering advice therefore runs the danger of assuming that all people's experiences of an event are the same when the reality is that different people who experience the same event often have radically different interpretations of it. So, offering advice can become dangerous because it may involve the caregiver projecting needs and solutions onto the care seeker rather than creating space for the care seeker to discern this themselves.

Another way caregivers may say too much is by turning the conversation to themselves. This occurs when the care seeker makes a disclosure and the caregiver responds by saying, "Oh yes, the same thing happened to me too—let me tell you all about it." There are many problems with this approach. First, it redirects the conversation onto the caregiver and away from the care seeker. This muddies the boundaries and purpose of the conversation because it calls into question who the focus of the conversation is and raises the possibility that the caregiver may need consolation from the care seeker. It also makes it more difficult for the caregiver to place the needs of the care seeker first—how can they, after all, if they're talking about themselves? Finally, the care seeker may not be prepared to hear anyone else's pain and suffering. The trauma they're experiencing may be quite enough, and so being forced to listen to someone else's disclosure can feel overwhelming. This can make the care seeker feel less safe as a result because they didn't consent to being in the role of listener when they sought out help.

Caregivers often take this approach in a conversation to create solidarity or to help the care seeker feel less alone. Put differently, it is an *attempt* to create more spiritual safety within the conversation, even though it results in less. Caregivers, therefore, may be well-intentioned, but sharing one's personal experience is rarely the most effective way to create a sense of safety or solidarity. Caregivers will likely be more effective through practices like asking open-ended questions, reflecting back what the care seeker has said, and listening more than they speak.

There is one other time when caregivers are apt to share their own experience of the trauma, and that is when care seekers directly ask about their relationship to it. In cases of collective trauma—like a hurricane that swept through their state or a gun shooting that happened in their neighborhood—the care seeker may want to know how the shared event affected the caregiver. In cases of seemingly individual trauma—including intimate partner violence or the untimely death of a loved one—care seekers may be searching for connection or understanding or simply be curious about the caregiver's personal history. In such instances, it may be tempting for a caregiver to answer directly because the care seeker asked. After all, if one of the goals of caregiving is to give agency back to the care seeker, then doesn't it thwart their agency to refuse to answer the question?

This may be too simple a resolution as to whether the caregiver should disclose, as there can be many ways to restore agency without doing so. Instead, it may be preferable for the caregiver to first find out *why* the care seeker is asking. It may be, for instance, that the care seeker wants to know whether the caregiver has direct experience of the trauma because they want to build trust with the caregiver. However, requesting details from the caregiver's personal life isn't necessary to that task; indeed, disclosing may ultimately make trust more difficult to build because the disclosure confuses the boundaries of the relationship. Caregivers should therefore do their best to discern the reason that the care seeker is asking the question, and then use caution combined with their best judgment to decide their own comfort with disclosure, first and foremost assessing whether sharing their own experience is in the best interest of the care seeker.

There is one way to disclose that may provide solidarity while not muddying the boundaries of the caregiving relationship, and that is to disclose outside of a caregiving situation. This is most easily done when a caregiver serves in contexts in which they have ongoing relationships with care seekers, such as in a church, school, or military unit. In these settings, a caregiver may be able to disclose details of their lives in educational forums, public advocacy work, or written publications. As a result, their history would be known to the care seeker *before* the care seeker comes for support and not disclosed during a caregiving session.

In such cases, the caregiver should nonetheless remember that it is their professional responsibility to put the needs of their care seekers first. Publicly disclosing a history of trauma can do enormous good for care seekers if it helps to dispel negative stereotypes about the trauma, ends a culture of silence, involves advocacy, or models hope. Conversely, it can also do damage if the caregiver is seeking personal attention or discloses so that their own emotional needs can be met by the community they are supposed to be serving. Caregivers should therefore do their own discernment work before making a public disclosure.

Finally, oversharing, offering advice, and other caregiver missteps often arise because the caregiver is uncomfortable in the conversation. They may be uncomfortable with vulnerability; perhaps the conversation triggers a prior trauma for them. Put more broadly, their own anxieties may rise to prominence during the conversation. In the moment, the caregiver may not be aware of the power that anxiety has and the way that it can lead to unhelpful responses, including disclosures, offering advice, or shutting down the conversation entirely. To avoid this, it is helpful for caregivers to engage in ongoing reflection about what brings them into a caregiving setting, how their own background shapes their responses, and what triggers certain responses in them. A skilled professional like a therapist or spiritual director can be helpful in doing this ongoing work, and caregivers will benefit from having this ongoing relationship and opportunity for reflection during their career. In addition, this work can also keep them from inadvertently harming those they seek to help.

Safe vs. Brave Spaces

A growing awareness of intersectional oppression has led to a critique of the concept of "safe spaces" in recent years, as theorists and activists alike have noted that there may never be truly safe spaces for difficult conversations, especially for those who face a combination of racism, sexism, classism, and ableism.[19] As a result, these experts aim not to find a completely safe space but rather to create a space in which people can be brave enough to speak despite the lack of safety.

This critique has validity, especially in relation to spaces involved in the criminal justice system, which all too often become sites of abuse for those who suffer from systemic oppression. However, safety needs to remain the priority and goal for trauma recovery and healthy spiritual care for several reasons. First, trauma survivors need more than the barest minimum when it comes to safety. Given their experiences and the emphasis placed upon safety for healing, they need robust safety across the board, including in matters of spiritual concern, and it falls to spiritual caregivers to ensure this. Second, the idea of brave spaces not only concedes that robust safety is impossible but it turns to the care seeker and requires them to be brave. Bravery might be appropriate to request in contexts unrelated to trauma, but asking a trauma survivor to be brave again on top of all they already suffered is like asking them to put on one more suit of armor because they must once again return to battle. Put differently, care seekers who struggle with trauma are vulnerable enough without spiritual caregivers asking them to be brave.

Instead of asking care seekers to be brave, caregivers can work to make their spaces safer for caregiving. Caregivers can provide more robust safety not only by engaging in some of the practices identified in this chapter but also by growing in their awareness about their own implicit biases and how those might affect their caregiving. They can also increase their awareness of how the systems around them may be promoting intersectional oppression so that they have a greater understanding of the barriers that care seekers face. That awareness, in turn, can help them engage more effectively in advocacy work to help end intersectional systemic oppression. Taking all these steps models a different way of being and acting in the world that is based upon placing the needs of care seekers first. Hence, even if safety cannot be guaranteed outside of the spiritual caregiving space, the efforts that a caregiver makes to ensure it nonetheless offers hope to the care seeker insofar as it lets them experience—in at least one context—the kind of safety that is ultimately needed for healing from trauma.

One might respond by proposing that asking spiritual caregivers to provide what society cannot is an unreasonable if not unrealistic request. Caregivers cannot transcend the norms or beliefs embedded within dominant culture, many of which are rooted in practices of intersectional systemic oppression and implicit bias. These forces are far greater than any individual caregiver. Asking them to do this work is therefore asking them to fail.

Yet while dominant culture in the United States certainly cannot be separated from embedded beliefs relating to intersectional systemic oppression, spiritual caregivers nonetheless have the skills to both build awareness of how these ideologies function and possess the ability to function as a prophetic presence in the lives of care seekers. After all, spiritual caregivers, at their best, have always made it their life's task to better the lives of care seekers, not to reinforce dominant ideologies about race, class, gender, and ability.[20] Indeed, one of the cornerstones of spiritual caregiving is that one places the needs of the most vulnerable first, recognizing that vulnerability is often constructed by culture's values. The way that spiritual caregiving is constructed as both within the world but apart from it therefore offers an opportunity for spiritual caregivers to work as prophets who model a different way of being, acting, and believing in the world. In so doing, they have the potential to carve out safe spaces for traumatized individuals to not only experience physical and spiritual groundedness, but also to speak freely about their experiences and find some meaning in them.

CHAPTER THREE

Meaning-Making

TRAUMA RECOVERY REQUIRES safety as its foundation, but once a survivor feels a reasonable degree of safety, then it becomes possible for them to begin to process their experiences to alleviate distress. Psychiatrist Judith Herman—who first proposed the three stages of trauma recovery—referred to the meaning-making stage as one in which two things occur: the person processes the trauma by *remembering* it, and the person processes the trauma by *mourning* what was lost due to it. Together, these two actions comprise the emotional, cognitive, and spiritual terrain of meaning-making.

Meaning-making is oftentimes one of the tasks that draws spiritual caregivers to their work. Indeed, we might consider it to be the work that involves the **spiritual processing** of an event.[1] Many spiritual caregivers find great joy and experience a sense of purpose in sharing the resources they have with distressed care seekers, and there are indeed many resources to share. When used well, the wisdom of the field can make a positive difference in the struggles care seekers face. Spiritual caregivers therefore play an important role at this stage of a trauma survivor's recovery, as they are often uniquely equipped to delve into struggles related to a care seeker's spiritual life. What follows, therefore, is a discussion of why meaning-making matters for healing, along with some tools that spiritual caregivers can bring to the task.

On Global and Situational Meaning

Humans are by and large meaning-making creatures, seeking to comprehend or structure their existence in a way that makes sense. One of the ways they do this is by developing a system of **global meaning.** Global meaning refers to a person's overall way of orienting the world around them or making sense of the world at large. A global system of meaning is essential for survival because it helps to structure or chunk phenomena that might otherwise seem chaotic or incomprehensible into something that appears to be consistent and reliable. Put differently, it is supposed to help a person find a sense of stability in the world.

One's global meaning system can come from many places. It might derive from a philosophy, like nihilism. It might also emerge directly from a religious system of knowledge. It may cobble together pieces of the two or develop independently. Psychologists find that global systems can either positively or negatively impact the way a person processes a given event, depending on whether the system is functioning as a helpful resource or a burden. In particular, they find that after a stressful event like a trauma, certain types of burdens are likely to exacerbate spiritual struggles, including an insecure relationship with the divine.[2]

Humans also assign meaning to specific events in their lives, in addition to formulating systems of global meaning. They may, for instance, assign meaning to mundane events, like a trip to the grocery store. They may also assign meaning to more significant events, like a milestone birthday or a death in the family. The way that a person appraises a situational event—or assigns **situational meaning**—may be consistent with their global system of meaning or inconsistent with it.[3] If it is consistent with the global system, then there is no reason for the person to feel a challenge posed to either their global or situational beliefs. However, they may find that the way they appraise the event is inconsistent with their global system of meaning. Such events thus pose a challenge to the person's global system of meaning, resulting in a **meaning-making clash** (see appendix B).[4]

Individuals who experience an event that they process as traumatic often identify those experiences as unfair, unpredictable, and uncontrollable.[5] As a result, they are precisely the kinds of events primed to challenge the perceived truth value of their global meaning-making system. In other words, if the purpose of a global system of meaning is to grant people ways of seeing their world that impose a sense of order in it, then trauma can represent the antithesis of that order. As a result, a clash emerges because either the person's global system of meaning is inaccurate, or the person is incapable of reliably appraising the trauma. Either way, it primes the person for distress, because they feel they've either misunderstood the world as they knew it, or they are no longer a reliable narrator of their own life.

One way to alleviate this distress is to help those who experience a trauma to reconcile the divergence between the trauma (situational meaning) and their global meaning. For an example of what this looks like, psychologists conducted a study of college students who had PTSD symptoms following exposure to an event that they described as particularly negative. The researchers found that when the students were able reconcile any discrepancy between their global meaning and the meaning they derived from the negative event, they were likely to experience an alleviation of PTSD symptoms.[6]

Embedded Beliefs and the Crisis of Meaning

Global beliefs encompass much, including one's gut sense of spirituality. They also can include embedded beliefs that were inherited as part of one's childhood belief system and that remained unexamined.[7] For instance, a person who grew up in the home of two Orthodox Jewish parents likely learned that God revealed important truths through the Torah. They also may have learned that it was important to keep kosher and that the weekly Shabbat celebration made each week rhythmical and predictable. Their parents also may have taught them that it was important for men and women to dress in certain kinds of clothing that represented their Orthodox faith commitments. In contrast, a person raised by an atheist single parent might have learned that God does not exist, and, therefore, that there is no reason to adhere to religious celebrations or rituals. The child's parent might also have taught them that humans have a responsibility to care for one another because they are inherently interconnected. That mandate to care, however, didn't come from the divine but from an inherent sense of what's right and wrong, according to the parent.

A person's embedded beliefs may come to be questioned at any point in life and give way to an intentionally chosen system of **deliberative beliefs.**[8] Deliberative beliefs may closely resemble one's embedded beliefs or be radically different from them, depending on how the process of questioning embedded beliefs resolves itself. In other words, a person might question their embedded beliefs and decide they still feel committed to most of them, or they may feel they no longer make sense and, as a result, they consciously embrace alternatives.

Traumas often call embedded beliefs into question. They may expose the ways in which they're life-limiting instead of life-giving, or they may seem to clash with the situational meaning that emerges after the trauma.[9] This can result in a *crisis of meaning* that specifically relates to a person's spiritual life. For instance, imagine a person who grew up in a religious tradition that taught them that God punishes people for doing bad things. This person experiences a negative event for which they were not responsible. Their embedded beliefs initially cause them to feel that they must have done something to deserve the trauma because, after all, people do not just experience harm for no reason. As a result, they feel ashamed and believe God must be punishing them, even though they cannot imagine why. However, as they continue to assess the trauma, they still cannot figure out why they are being punished. This causes them to begin to question their embedded beliefs about a punishing God because those beliefs no longer make sense in light of the trauma. As a result, they develop a deliberative theology in which they no longer believe in God. This example shows how the hypothetical person observed a clash between their embedded beliefs and the situational meaning they ascribed to the trauma, and then they resolved that clash by revising their beliefs about God. In this case, then, the trauma held greater sway in terms of authoritative knowledge for the person than their embedded beliefs did.

Now imagine, by way of contrast, that the hypothetical person was unable to reconcile the embedded belief they had about God with the situational meaning they developed about the trauma. Psychologists recognize that such situations are more likely to result in rumination and distressing symptoms that are part of the PTSD cluster. This makes sense because the person hasn't resolved the meaning-making conflict into a part of their life's story, and so it continues to occupy their mind and body, either consciously or unconsciously, as a set of conflicting parts rather than a whole. Bringing together those parts into a whole is often described as a process of **integration.**[10] Without integration, it can be very difficult for a person or community to move past the trauma they experienced.

Meaning making is also part of **post-traumatic growth**. Post-traumatic growth is different from resilience. Whereas resilience involves the ability to bounce back, post-traumatic growth describes the growth that occurs when one struggles to bounce back. Experts believe this growth occurs across five domains, namely: (1) an appreciation for one's life, (2) an awareness of new possibilities, (3) new ways of relating to others, (4). an awareness of one's personal strength, and (5) changes and growth in one's spirituality.

Meaning making can assist with growth across these five domains, even when suffering is ongoing. It is also likely that meaning making will continue to occur after suffering subsides. Meaning making therefore allows people to resolve distress that emerges from the trauma so that they can become integrated, whole selves, even as it can also occur in the midst of suffering.

Listen, Assess, Cocreate

Healing is more likely to occur in trauma when survivors find ways to resolve meaning-making struggles, or, put differently, when they find ways of conceptualizing the trauma that make sense in the narrative of their life.[11] Pastoral theologian Carrie Doehring writes that caregivers can play an essential role in this process by engaging in the threefold stages of *listening*, *assessing*, and *cocreating*. Doehring's is a fundamentally narrative approach, meaning that it acknowledges that humans are by nature embodied stories (as discussed in chapter 1) and that the best forms of spiritual care create a safe space for story telling as well as a trustworthy space in which the story's meaning can be constructed so people can make sense of their lives. It is also an attempt to embed Judith Herman's three stages—safety, meaning-making, and reconnection—within a process of holistic care that ultimately helps a person to resolve meaning-making clashes and alleviate spiritual distress. One can observe this by noting how the three stages function: When caregivers actively listen to care seekers, they offer a spiritually safe space for sharing the story of the harm (see chapter 2 for more information on safety). When caregivers engage in assessment, they take that initial narrative—however fractured it may be—that a trauma survivor offers and assist with helping to identify what a person's embedded beliefs are, where the struggles may be, and what resources exist to resolve them. This second step therefore becomes the heart of the meaning-making process. That process continues in the cocreate stage, a relational process that relies upon trust and that facilitates reconnection. A more detailed consideration of how spiritual caregivers can employ each step follows below.

Listening

The first stage—listening—involves creating enough safety for care seekers to share their story. In this way, caregivers may serve as *witnesses* to the trauma. Trauma theorists find that speaking about trauma does something to how trauma functions in the body and narrative of survivors.[12] Offering a *testimony* of the harm done, therefore, makes concrete the sadness, injustice, and anger wrought by the event in a way that trusted others can receive and validate.[13]

Speaking about the trauma is one way of offering a testimony. When individuals speak about the trauma, they may tell a story that is easy to follow, but it may also be fragmented, nonlinear, and filled with gaps. The person may have very detailed memories of some aspects of the trauma that seem peripheral to it, just as they may be unable to remember core aspects of it. In some cases, they may have no direct memory of it at all. All of this is typical of how traumatic memories encode in the brain.

Survivors may also have trouble speaking about the trauma, even when they do remember it. The inability to speak also has to do with the way that trauma encodes in the brain, as explained in chapter 1. If speech is difficult for the care seeker, it may be because they feel emotionally overwhelmed by the event; however, it may also be the case that they feel that speech fails to capture the event. As a result, some care seekers may find that other creative ways of offering testimony feel more authentic or are more cathartic ways of telling the trauma's story. Poetry, art, and music can all provide opportunities for telling the story of the trauma in a way that helps to remember and mourn it. Caregivers can benefit from greater knowledge and experience in the arts so that they can assist care seekers in using them (see appendix A for suggestions).

Regardless of how trauma survivors choose to share their stories, caregivers who listen should employ the best practices of their field. These include **active listening**, which involves giving one's full attention to what is being said. The caregiver who listens actively is not evaluating or preparing a response while the care seeker speaks. They are also observing the contents of what the care seeker says as well as their tone of voice, facial expressions, and body language. Active listening also involves the ability to listen into the unique context of the care seeker's life. For instance, a person with autism may not make eye contact when they speak. A caregiver who doesn't know that autistic individuals often feel uncomfortable making eye contact may think the care seeker is ashamed instead of recognizing that it is the most comfortable way for them to communicate.

The orientation that a care seeker brings to the task of active listening also matters. When working with trauma survivors, caregivers will benefit from utilizing both a **hermeneutic of belief** and **unconditional positive regard**. A hermeneutic of belief means that a caregiver comes to the conversation assuming belief or, put in more technical terms, employing a method of listening that is predicated upon belief in what the care seeker shares. As stated in chapter 2, trauma survivors often face barriers to others believing them, so when caregivers assume belief, they remove some of the burden from the care seeker. Instead of having to be on the offensive—of having to convince others that their testimony is true—they can simply say what is in their hearts.

Likewise, unconditional positive regard can help a care seeker feel safe and brave enough to share their story. Unconditional positive regard is a technique in which the caregiver displays total acceptance and support of the care seeker, without that acceptance and support being dependent on what they do or say. Caregivers who offer unconditional positive regard signal several things. First, they communicate that the care seeker has *essentially positive value*, meaning that their worth as a human being isn't dependent on their actions, beliefs, feelings, or the things that they've experienced. Instead, their positive worth emerges from their identity—from the fact that they are here as human beings in this particular form. Additionally, caregivers who offer unconditional positive regard signal that there is no shame in difficult feelings. Oftentimes, the norms of Western, white society have communicated to care seekers that there is shame in strong or negative emotions. Men often learn from an early age that there is shame in expressing emotions like sadness—which includes crying—because sadness conveys vulnerability, and men are not supposed to be vulnerable. Conversely, women often inherit the belief from an early age that they should not display anger because anger is a strong, aggressive emotion, and the proper woman is neither strong nor aggressive. The problem, of course, is that traumas usually bring in their wake feelings like sadness and anger, and if individuals do not believe that such feelings are safe to either possess or express, then they may feel ashamed of their feelings *and* try to stifle them.

All of this is problematic for healing because emotions do not just disappear. Much like a cup being filled with water, the feelings will continue to accumulate until they overflow and cause a mess. As a result, it becomes important for individuals to find ways to process their emotions, instead of letting them pile up. When a caregiver displays unconditional positive regard, therefore, they signal that such emotions are okay to share within the context of the relationship which, in turn, helps the care seeker reframe the moral value of their feelings. As a result, the care seeker may feel safe enough to process and, eventually, move beyond difficult feelings without shame. Doing so, in turn, increases their self-worth. As their self-worth grows, care seekers may feel greater confidence as well as greater agency.

In addition to utilizing a hermeneutic of belief and unconditional positive regard, there are two practical skills that a caregiver can employ in the task of active listening. The first is that they can *paraphrase* what the care seeker shared. Paraphrasing allows the caregiver to *rephrase* the care seeker's reflections so that they can hear them for themselves. Paraphrasing also allows a caregiver to *clarify* anything that might be unclear or to *summarize* main points of what the care seeker spoke as a means of reinforcement. In addition, they can observe the care seeker's *body language* during the conversation. Body language can signal how comfortable the care seeker is during the conversation. For instance, a care seeker who curls up in a ball or who keeps clenching their fists may be experiencing stress during the conversation. In contrast, a care seeker who leans back in their chair, keeping their hands on their lap and maintaining eye contact throughout the conversation, is likely more comfortable. Caregivers benefit from noticing such cues so that they can take steps to ensure that care seekers remain grounded in the conversation.

As caregivers listen, they may also observe that it can be difficult for individuals to speak about the trauma. Recall from chapter 1 that this makes sense, given how trauma encodes in the brain. Recall also that it is not necessary for caregivers to know details of the trauma (Auden's Rule) in order to offer excellent care. What is necessary is to create a space that feels safe for care seekers to share what they feel needs to be shared to remember and mourn the event and to begin to find some meaning in it.

Assessing and Cocreating

In the assessing stage, the caregiver begins to systematically evaluate the effect of the trauma on the care seeker's spiritual life.[14] They may want to undertake a formal assessment that helps them evaluate a person's spiritual background and current beliefs and practices, or, for a very simple tool, they might consider what is commonly referred to as the FICA screen (appendix C). The FICA tool is composed of four questions that help caregivers get a sense of a person's current spiritual life as well as their spiritual background, embedded beliefs, and resources. It can be helpful in giving caregivers a sense of how the person's global system of meaning is functioning in relation to the trauma and whether there are clashes between it and the situational meaning of the trauma.

Assessment tools like the FICA may seem cold or impersonal to caregivers, but one of their benefits is that they can ensure that caregivers receive necessary information about a person's spiritual life. In cases of trauma, it may also be helpful for the caregiver to learn more about the person's background, including their *family system*, in order to gain a greater sense of how their embedded beliefs emerged within it, and the extent to which those beliefs are life-giving or life-limiting. Questions about a person's embedded beliefs can also help to reveal clashes between the care seeker's global meaning and the meaning they've attributed to the traumatic situation.

The purpose of the assessment stage is to help the caregiver gain clarity on what might be needed for the care seeker to alleviate spiritual distress. Because meaning-making is essential to this process of alleviating distress, the information that one receives in the assessment stage can then be brought into the cocreate stage, where the care seeker and caregiver together undertake agreed upon actions to help the care seeker to regain agency through the process of participating in meaning-building activities. For instance, care seekers might find the opportunity to engage in a *ritual* meaningful.[15] Rituals are structured activities that follow a predetermined order and that often have an element of history to them. Rituals can memorialize or mark the end of something, like a funeral or graduation does. They can also mark the beginning of an event, like a briss, bar mitzvah, or bat mitzvah does in the Jewish tradition. Rituals can mark a celebration—such as the recitation of the *Shahada* does in Islam—or they can be sites of lament.

Rituals may also be either private or public. Examples of private rituals include the saying of the rosary in Roman Catholicism or meditating in Buddhism. Examples of public rituals include the *Kumbha Mela*—a mass Hindu pilgrimage to one of four Indian rivers—as well as smaller public events like weddings and funerals.

One of the benefits of a ritual is that it might help a care seeker speak about, remember, and mourn the trauma via a structured, predictable liturgy.[16] If the person is part of a religious tradition, they may want to undertake a meaningful ritual that is already part of their tradition. For instance, if a care seeker who has a strong relationship to their religious tradition lost a loved one in a trauma, they may find it meaningful to memorialize them with a well-worn funeral service that comes directly from their tradition. The care seeker may already know the prayers in this funeral because they've attended others during the course of their lifetime, and so the words are comforting because they are familiar. For many Christians, The Lord's Prayer or Psalm 23 are examples of this—both are often comforting because they're known by heart and have a long tradition in the ritual lives of Christian care seekers. Care seekers who are committed to their religious tradition might also choose hymns that they've known from heart since childhood. Again, for Christians, hymns like "Amazing Grace" are often comforting because they are known so well. A funeral ritual that is organized in a comforting, familiar way may help the care seeker in their meaning-making efforts because it allows them to access the religious tradition that brings them a sense of spiritual safety because it is familiar. As a result, they experience the prayers and music as life-giving instead of life-limiting. The ritual thus helps frame and grant meaning to the trauma in light of the religious tradition that the person experiences as life-giving.

In contrast, the trauma survivor might feel very differently about the funeral if they have a negative relationship to the religious tradition of their childhood. They may find the idea of a funeral important but want to do something that is entirely separate from what they grew up knowing. Alternatively, they may want to keep some elements that feel life-giving—like the structure of the service or a specific prayer or hymn—and discard the parts that are life-limiting. They feel that with a bit of help, they could develop a funeral ritual that is both intentional and true to the beliefs of themselves and their family. Caregivers can help care seekers to develop such a ritual using several steps. First, they can begin by asking about what is meaningful and incorporating it in a way that makes sense. This step involves assessing what is needed from the ritual in order to help resolve distress in the care seeker.

After caregivers do this assessment work, they can then begin to develop the ritual by drawing on spiritual resources that will help with the meaning-making task. This step might involve drawing on prayers and music for rituals that resonate because of the care seeker's previous history with them. It might also involve developing new ones. Likely, it will involve conversations with the care seeker about their history with the elements of the ritual. Having done this—or, perhaps, jointly with it—caregivers will want to partner with the care seeker to decide on a structure for the ritual. They might either create or use a preexisting one. The caregiver will also want to ensure that all elements of the ritual facilitate connection between the care seeker and their community. To that end, caregivers will want to make sure they understand how care seekers imagine the community being engaged in the ritual itself. Finally, they will want to integrate additional diverse spiritual resources as needed.[17]

In cases of trauma, rituals can help people structure their *lament*, meaning that they assist in the process of expressing grief and loss. As Judith Herman notes, this process of mourning is essential to the task of meaning-making in trauma. It helps care seekers realize what was lost in the trauma and what has shifted because of it. Ritualized forms of lament are central in virtually all religious traditions and are also represented in religious texts. Care seekers may consider drawing on the resources of their own traditions, including the preexisting rituals and texts that feel meaningful to them. Alternatively, they may want to develop new rituals alongside the caregiver to help them formally both *remember* and *mourn* what the trauma caused them to lose.

One of the benefits of a ritual is that it often utilizes previously developed language, including prayers, hymns, readings, popular songs, and poems. This takes some of the burden off the care seeker to find the words to describe both the harm and the need to lament it. Instead, the care seeker can hopefully find solidarity in the words of those who came before them, whether they are the well-worn words of a Scripture passage or more recently penned words, including songs, poems, or even reflections that the care seeker wrote in advance of the service.

Rituals also help participants to enter into liminal spaces.[18] A **liminal space** is a transitional space, a space not meant to be permanently inhabited. Physical examples of liminal spaces include hospitals, elevators, bridges, airports, and churches. When people step into any of these places, they enter a location intended to be passed through. One drives onto a bridge to get to the other side, just as one steps into an airport with the goal of departing on a plane and landing somewhere else. Physically liminal spaces can also lead to an emotional, cognitive, or spiritual transition. For instance, when a pregnant woman enters labor and goes to the hospital, that liminal space facilitates her transition to motherhood. Likewise, when a seeker sits in a church pew, they remove themselves purposefully from the material world in order to encounter the divine and then return to the material world changed by that encounter.

While liminal spaces can be physical, they can also be emotional, cognitive, or spiritual. Indeed, trauma survivors often find themselves occupying emotionally and spiritually liminal spaces. They often feel that they are inhabiting these spaces because of the questions raised by the event or because of the crisis of meaning that erupted due to the clash of situational and global meaning. Additionally, trauma survivors may feel that they've entered a liminal space because of how the trauma challenges assumptions about their self-concept, as they no longer feel like they are the same person that they were before the trauma. They may, for instance, be struggling with labels like, "survivor" and "victim." It may be the case that neither resonates, or it may be that the person feels they never consented to be a person whose identity incorporated the trauma, as was the case with Chanel Miller in chapter 1. These kinds of liminal spaces can feel destabilizing to the care seeker because they may sense that their prior beliefs or life is no longer the right "fit," but they also lack a clear sense of what comes next.

While liminality can feel discomfiting or unsettling, it is also a space where spiritual growth can occur. Spiritual caregivers have several resources to help facilitate this growth, which may be best integrated into the co-create stage. These strategies can also help facilitate remembrance and mourning, both of which—as Judith Herman recognized—are central to the meaning-making process.

Meaning-Making in Traumatic Moral Injury

Moral injury occurs when an experience violates someone's sense of right and wrong. Moral injury was initially described with military settings in mind and specifically combat experiences that required lethal use of force. Members of the military commit to following a chain of command that requires them to carry out orders as a unit, often in ambiguous circumstances that involve immediate action. As a result, they may have to do certain acts that, especially over time, generate guilt, shame, betrayal, and self-disgust. However, moral injury is not limited to military settings and can occur anywhere. During the peak of the Covid-19 crisis, for instance, hospital staff sometimes had to make and follow triage orders that required them to place the medical needs of some individuals above others. They also had to watch decisions being made that they felt were wrong but over which they had no control. Though they may have had a different view of what appropriate care required, they were not given an opportunity to exercise that belief, which may have resulted in moral injury. Likewise, in business and school settings, employees may be unable to carry out their own beliefs because of the directions of their bosses. As a result, they may make choices that they regret or that compromise their core beliefs and values.

Moral injuries can be traumatic. This creates a complicated situation for caregivers, who must both navigate issues related to the trauma and issues emerging from the moral injury. As a hypothetical example, one might imagine a military chaplain caring for a soldier who recently returned from a war. As part of a military operation, the soldier witnessed several of their own colleagues being shot by a sniper. The soldier received orders to shoot the sniper, who was an adolescent. The soldier successfully shot and killed the sniper, but now feels guilt and shame, knowing that the sniper was likely coerced into the role to begin with. The soldier therefore feels several conflicting feelings, while also feeling the effects more generally associated with trauma.

In such cases, caregivers can first help by explaining that what the care seeker is experiencing involves trauma and moral injury. Additional support from a therapist is likely needed, though the spiritual caregiver can still play an important role in the meaning-making process by offering not only opportunities for lament but also opportunities for the care seeker to make things right and to resolve the conflicts between their global worldview and the conflicts posed by this given situation.[19]

Meaning-Making in Intergenerational Trauma

Intergenerational trauma poses a unique set of meaning-making challenges. The distress that care seekers experience is vicarious—a kind of secondary trauma—and, in turn, it is also impossible to access, to touch, or to realize because the care seeker is separated from the trauma by time (assuming that the trauma itself has ended and is not ongoing across generations). The story is simultaneously theirs and not theirs. The history belongs to them, or perhaps it would be more aptly said that the history was thrust upon them. The physical experience of the event does not.

The practical resources available to caregivers described in the previous sections can be employed in intergenerational trauma. The process of listening, assessing, and cocreating can be utilized, and the use of the arts and ritual remain helpful resources for remembrance and mourning. The return of agency remains paramount, as does the need for some kind of meaning to be derived from the event. In addition to these tasks, intergenerational trauma requires a unique kind of identity work, as the care seeker must find ways to separate their own identity from the legacy of trauma so that the trauma becomes a meaningful part of the past but not the entirety of their present. In this way, care seekers will benefit from finding ways to both name the trauma's impact while also finding ways to form their own story apart from its ongoing legacy.

As care seekers differentiate from prior generations, they may find it helpful to question the embedded beliefs that they inherited from prior generations. For instance, if prior generations lived in a dangerous environment, they may have developed a practice of never asking for help because it was too unsafe to do so. That belief may have been passed from parent to child, down to the current generation. While this form of coping may have initially served a purpose—to protect the generation that was in danger—it may now cause problems, assuming that the trauma has ended. In this case, never asking for help can sow seeds of distrust and foreclose the possibility of meaningful relationships developing. The inability to ask for help may likewise keep individuals from seeking out effective care. As in cases of primary trauma, therefore, caregivers can help care seekers by raising awareness about how the inheritance of embedded beliefs may be resulting in distress or a meaning-making clash.[20]

The Danger of Clichés and Interpretation

Caregivers can make several mistakes during the meaning-making stage. One is to respond with clichés or prepackaged interpretations when offering meaning to the care seeker. This practice is problematic for several reasons: First, it robs the care seeker of narrative agency. Recall that care seekers often lose agency in the trauma, causing them to feel helpless or chaotic. One of the goals of healing is, therefore, to reclaim it. However, when a caregiver provides an interpretation or purpose for the trauma, then they've unwittingly prevented that from happening.

A second reason that providing interpretations is so problematic is that it's speculative. In other words, the caregiver simply cannot know for sure that their interpretation is correct. By way of example, consider this story from philosopher Susan Brison's book *Aftermath*, in which she documents some of her own recovery from a physically violent rape and attempted murder. Brison writes that after her attack, her aunt wrote her a belated birthday card in which she stated that she was sure the rape and attempted murder would help her "become stronger" and "able to help so many people. A real blessing from above for sure."[21] But was it a real blessing from above? How could Brison's aunt be so certain?

Brison's aunt may have been offering this interpretation to avoid her own discomfort with what happened to her niece. Put differently, it's possible that the meaning she imposed was aimed more at meeting her own needs than it was at helping Brison. She therefore wasn't functioning in a way that would be considered other-directed. Alternatively, however, Brison's aunt may very much have believed in a worldview in which the meaning and purpose of negative experiences is to help individuals grow, even if that's not what Brison's experience was revealing. She certainly wouldn't be the only person to hold this perspective—Christian theologians have proposed twists on this kind of theodicy for centuries.[22]

There are some benefits to letting a theory pre-determine the meaning of trauma. First, it means that a person doesn't have to search for meaning; the meaning is already present and easily accessible. Drawing from pre-existing theories of why negative things occur therefore has some ease to it, and it may even be comforting if it truly aligns with what one believes and feels in their body.

The problem, of course, is that humans don't live in theory. They live in practice and as such, they encounter realities that are messier than what theories can accommodate. So, when meaning gets imposed by theory alone, then it runs the danger of becoming an idol rather than a source of wisdom, something that one attempts to conform and contort experience to instead of something that emerges from the experience itself.

An Exception to the Rule

There is one time, however, where it may be helpful for caregivers to provide a sense of direction or meaning, and this has to do with validating the harm of the trauma. Care seekers may struggle with issues related to validation during the meaning-making stage. One reason this occurs is that individuals may feel unentitled to see themselves as someone who experienced a trauma, especially in the United States, where Western, white culture has made it inappropriate to share vulnerable feelings and experiences. Alternatively, they may feel unentitled to do so because they feel the trauma wasn't "bad" enough, compared to what they see on television or what they've heard about from other people they know. Compared to others, they may say, what they encountered isn't so bad. This may occur especially in cases of vicarious trauma or in cases where trauma doesn't seem to fit stereotypes.

Caregivers can help in such cases by validating the person's experience or by giving a name to that which seems beyond categorization. Here is an example of how to do this: In a case where a caregiver observes that a person keeps saying the event wasn't a big deal because many other people suffer worse harms, the caregiver might say something simple like, "What you describe sounds to me like a trauma. How does it feel when I say that?"

In this example, the caregiver is using the power of their caregiving role to validate the care seeker's experience.[23] However, they are still giving the care seeker an opportunity to respond and wrestle with the idea, rather than imposing the identity on them in the way that a doctor imposes a diagnosis. In this way, the caregiver is also using their authority to hand some agency back to the care seeker.

Hearing themselves described as someone who lived through a trauma, perhaps as a "victim" or "survivor," can be challenging for the care seeker, especially if they have been in denial. However, wrestling for meaning is significantly harder without a name for what one has experienced.[24] As a result, naming can ultimately be helpful for the care seeker in the tasks of remembering, mourning, and integrating the trauma into the narrative of their life. It can also be necessary for the process of reconnecting.

CHAPTER FOUR

Reconnection

Introduction

TRAUMA CHALLENGES A person's sense of safety, their understanding of their own identity, and their relationship to the world around them. Reconnection involves the process of integrating one's reconfigured identity into their community in the aftermath of a trauma. In other words, having become grounded in safety, having mourned and found some meaning in the trauma, survivors can now integrate the event into their sense of self, resulting in a new self-concept. They can also develop new relationships, discover anew what their beliefs are, and create a new future for themselves.[1] These three tasks—developing a new self, creating a new future, and discovering new relationships—thereby involve both reconnecting with the fullness of one's posttraumatic self as well as reconnecting with one's community.

Judith Herman writes that if the core elements of trauma are helplessness and isolation, then reconnection counters those with empowerment and renewed relationships.[2] This process of reconnection often involves skills related to **resiliency**, meaning skills that allow someone to adapt after trauma and engage in post-traumatic growth, which psychologists understand as positive transformation that can occur in the aftermath of a trauma.[3] Spiritual caregivers can assist in these three elements of the reconnective process by providing resources to support both the process of reconnecting with one's self and with others.

Reconnecting with One's Self

Prior chapters explored how trauma can appear to call into question or even destroy the survivor's sense of self-concept. They may question their physical safety, their moral choices, the purpose of their lives, and who they are in relation to others. The meaning-making stage helps resolve clashes that emerge between global frameworks of meaning and the trauma. The wisdom gained in this stage begins to be applied in the reconnection stage, as the care seeker becomes more deeply acquainted with the new sense of self that emerged because of the safety and meaning-making steps.

Physical, psychological, and spiritual empowerment can be core elements of this process. Many survivors find that writing is a helpful way to reconnect with one's self in the aftermath of trauma. Writing is a private endeavor, which makes it a safe forum for individuals to express things to the paper that they might not feel comfortable sharing with another person. Writing can also be changed—words can be crossed out; entire paragraphs and pages can be rewritten. The ability to change the writing helps the survivor reclaim agency by putting them in control of what stays and what goes. Writing can also be a helpful way for the survivor to reflect on how the trauma has affected their sense of self and the narrative of their life. Keeping a journal likewise can be useful because it can offer a safe and private way to do this work. It can also provide a record of the journey over time, so that they can better understand how their sense of self and the meaning they derived from the trauma changed. Other art forms—including painting and dance—may help with this task as well.

Survivors also can reconnect with themselves by finding ways to reconnect with their bodies. Care seekers may benefit from participating in regular practices that help them to listen to what their body needs and what it is feeling. Mindfulness practices like contemplative prayer and guided or non-guided meditation can assist with this. Yoga is also helpful for many people who want to engage in a body-based spiritual practice.

Additionally, traumatized individuals may also find it helpful to become more aware of potential triggers and how to helpfully respond to them. A therapist may be particularly skilled in assisting with this task, although this is still something survivors can develop on their own by keeping a record of times they were triggered and times when they found ways to constructively respond or avoid the trigger. This record can help them understand the patterns of their own responses so that they can grow in awareness of both their triggers and the resources they have to avoid or respond to them. Ultimately, this gives survivors a greater tool kit for their own thriving.

More generally, survivors will benefit from taking time to identify the emotions they're feeling and what their body needs at any given time. This kind of mindfulness can help survivors better understand their own needs and to support those needs instead of avoiding or negatively judging them. Additionally, services like massage and reiki can help trauma survivors reconnect with their body in a safe environment.

One of the other things that care seekers may do as an embodied practice is to find ways to feel their own power and strength. This can be especially valuable because traumas often highlight human vulnerability. While strength-based practices do not eradicate vulnerability, they can be opportunities for survivors to reclaim agency by recognizing that they do have a strength of their own. One way that survivors may do this is by doing more strength training activities, like lifting weights or high-intensity interval training (HIIT). Other care seekers may choose to take self-defense lessons to strengthen their ability to fight in the case of a future trauma, especially in cases where they felt physically unable to defend themselves in the past. Programs like Smart Defense—the self-defense program started by kidnapping and rape survivor Elizabeth Smart—recognize that disempowerment is often a reason individuals enroll in the course, and so one of the goals is to give students practical skills that will help them feel stronger in the world.

The process of reconnecting with one's self can be a challenging one. The survivor may feel a sense of shame because of their own vulnerability or because of the difficult emotions that the trauma brings up. It can therefore be easy for the negative voices in the survivor's head to take over. I once had a colleague who called these voices "inner gremlins" because they could be so negative and insidious. One way that pastoral caregivers may be able to help survivors who battle their own inner gremlins is to remind them that these voices do not deserve the power they want to exert. Instead, survivors can benefit by recognizing that this inner monologue—this negative self-talk—does not represent the fullness of who they are. It doesn't even represent a fraction of it. So, one way to respond to these gremlins is to acknowledge their presence but not their power, to say, "Okay, so you think I should never leave the house because I have no worth, but today I'm going to try something different and go to the mall." Individuals may also want to keep a log of the negative self-talk in order to become more aware of those thoughts and to challenge them. Caregivers may be helpful in identifying the shame, fear, and pessimism that the gremlins often represent. They may also be able to help by reminding the care seeker that because they have value and worth (or, put into theological language, because they are a beloved child of God), these voices do not speak the truth.

Counterintuitively, humor can be a way to disarm the inner gremlins. By identifying what they're saying and turning it into something lighthearted, it robs them of their power. Reframing the negative beliefs of the gremlins as positives can also be a helpful way for the care seeker to reclaim their sense of worth. Care seekers can do this work on their own, or with friends, spiritual care givers, and therapists.

Reconnecting with One's Community

The survivor begins to rewrite the narrative of their life in this stage of trauma, beginning with the process of reconnecting with their own renewed sense of identity and purpose. The trust they developed in the prior two stages builds the foundation of this process of recovery, which then gets extended into the task of reconnecting with others. Spiritual care providers can assist in this task in many ways. First, they can affirm the relational work the survivor is doing. For instance, it is not uncommon for survivors in this stage to seek out partnerships, to work to strengthen their existing relationships, or to consider starting a family. Such relationships require not only trust but also the capacity for emotional intimacy. They can affirm the bravery it takes to undertake these tasks, should the survivor choose to do so. It is important, however, that the caregiver does not direct the care seeker because, as in other areas of trauma recovery, the act of choosing to pursue relationships offers the chance to reclaim agency that was lost in the trauma. The act of being told to do so takes that agency away.

This may also be the stage where care seekers begin to reconnect with their relationship to the divine. This process may involve a return to one's prior faith tradition, or it may involve a burgeoning new faith. Either way, the hope is that the belief system that the care seeker carries at this stage of the journey is rooted in deliberative beliefs derived during the meaning-making stage, when the care seeker did the hard work of reconsidering their embedded beliefs in light of the trauma. Care seekers can assist in this stage by reflecting back what they hear the care seeker saying about their spiritual journey and by affirming the steps they've taken so far. Now is not the time to try to convert care seekers or to try to persuade them to relate to the divine in a certain way. Rather, caregivers will be best served at this stage by using the same listening skills employed in the prior two steps of recovery, thereby allowing the care seeker to identify, wrestle with, and ultimately find comfort in the belief system they've chosen for themselves.

Care seekers in this stage may also benefit from building relationships in their faith communities. This may be, for instance, the first time that a care seeker becomes involved in an organized religion, or it may be that the care seeker chooses to return to a faith tradition they left during this stage. The spiritual caregiver can help the care seeker by offering appropriate spiritual resources for this stage of the journey. These may include twelve-step programs or support groups that may or may not be run by the organization where the spiritual caregiver works. To that end, it is helpful for spiritual caregivers to be aware of the resources in their area, so that they can offer these relationship-building resources to care seekers.

Individuals may also begin to disclose the trauma more openly to family, friends, and their wider community at this time. This can be an empowering process, as it allows the survivor to act as a truth teller and gives them a sense of freedom because they are no longer bound by holding the trauma as a secret. They may also feel a renewed sense of trust in members of their community if they experience disclosure as a time when the people they care about believed them.

However, one of the struggles care seekers may face in this process is that they do not have control over how members of their community will respond to them, and they may face barriers for a number of reasons. First, members of their community may see them as an unreliable narrator of the story. In cases of childhood abuse, for instance, the care seeker may be accused of misremembering because of their age. In cases of gender-based violence against women, care seekers may be accused of inviting the wrong due to how they were dressed, because of prior sexual activity, or because of levels of intoxication. In cases where the care seeker is not white, the social construction of their race may cause listeners to see them as incapable of being victimized.

The sheer amount of what is at stake in believing survivors may also compound the task of disclosing. A survivor who makes an accusation against a parent, for instance, is asking other family members to radically reconfigure their relationship to and the trust they placed in the accused. Sometimes, this may be too big of an ask for the people who hear the disclosure, and they either consciously or unconsciously find it easier to dismiss the claim than to do the hard work of questioning their own choices and beliefs. Survivors face similar barriers when making accusations against religious leaders and the institutions they represent. In such cases, faith communities may be more apt to rally around the perpetrating party than the victimized one for several reasons. As in the case of family members, members of religious communities may find it too big of an ask to question them. In organizations that hold a high ontology of leaders—meaning they hold leaders in high regard or put them on a pedestal—it may be unfathomable to believe that such wrongdoing could occur. Moreover, if listeners did believe it, then they could be ostracized or punished by the institution—in other words, the risk of believing the survivor may feel too great to listeners.

The institution itself may also refuse to take survivor accusations seriously for the simple reason that they have too much to lose.

They may fear a loss of integrity or public opinion or widespread trust. They may fear the money they would lose if survivors filed lawsuits. They may fear all of the above and more. As a result, religious organizations have an unfortunate tendency to close ranks in cases where survivors make allegations of abuse, thereby causing survivors to feel unheard. For just a smattering of examples, see Brigham Young University's response to Mormon students who alleged rape occurred on campus, Scientology's treatment of former members who dared to speak about alleged abuses throughout the leadership ranks, Liberty University's attempts to silence victims of sexual assault, and the Roman Catholic Church's response to international allegations of abuse, which involved gaslighting and ostracizing victims, while moving priests to different parishes instead of accepting accountability and engaging in meaningful accountability for wrongdoing. Those who experience trauma at the hands of organizations—including religious institutions—are thereby justified in their fear that the cost of coming forward may be too high.

Spiritual caregivers can play an important role in supporting care seekers who are considering making an accusation against an institution or who have done so. One way they can help is by reminding the survivor that no one should ever be forced to make a disclosure, that the risks of doing so are real and that only they can decide whether they want to take on those risks. In cases where survivors do decide to move forward with allegations, spiritual caregivers can support survivors in the effort by continuing to believe them, even as others may call their validity into question. They may want to help the survivor find alternative communities of support to counter the ostracization they may experience as a result of the disclosure. Finally, they can help the survivor to identify how the act of disclosure itself is an empowering act of reclaiming agency. While survivors cannot control the outcome, they can hold onto the disclosure as an example of how they are countering the helplessness and isolation of the trauma with acts of agency, integrity, and truth telling that ultimately help to place the trauma, rightfully, into the past instead of the present.

Reconnection and Justice

Many survivors engage fully in the process of reconnection through their immediate relationships. However, some feel that part of the reconnection process involves a more sustained effort to engage in justice work around the trauma. This might involve volunteering with a local non-profit that focuses its efforts on eradicating the trauma, helping other survivors, or telling one's story in a more public way to raise awareness about the type of trauma they experienced or to provide ideas for how to end its prevalence. Elizabeth Smart, described in earlier chapters of this book, is one example of an individual who engaged in public advocacy work in the aftermath of her kidnapping. Since that event, she has started a non-profit organization dedicated to ending sexual assault and crimes against children. She also hosts a podcast to raise awareness about sexual violations and developed the Smart Defense program. Similarly, Chanel Miller—quoted in chapter 2—not only wrote about the sexual violation she suffered but also published the account as a memoir which raised awareness about how the justice system fails to meet the needs of survivors. Such examples are public ones that turned the survivor into a household name. However, this form of reconnection work does not necessarily have to be so high profile. It may be local, grassroots, and rooted in relationships formed with members of one's community. In this way, the survivor makes a difference by seeking to transform the world around them from one in which injustice goes unnoted and unaddressed to one in which it may be transformed or ended entirely.

One struggle that survivors may run into at this stage is that they may feel disheartened that their efforts do not always result in concrete change. Indeed, they know firsthand how devastating specific forms of trauma can be, and therefore, they bring a personal passion for eradicating them *and* a desire to end them as soon as possible. When individuals or systems thwart that process, survivors may feel disheartened or may doubt the people and power structures that prevent change from occurring. Spiritual caregivers can help by providing a *ministry of presence*. In practicing this ministry, caregivers offer solidarity rather than advice and presence instead of problem-solving so that care seekers can feel heard, validated, and strengthened.

Resolution

Judith Herman writes that trauma is never fully resolved, never entirely complete.[4] The survivor who emerges from the initial safety and meaning-making stages may have a triggering moment that causes them to reassess the prior two stages anew. Spiritual caregivers can help by educating people about how trauma works so that a return to earlier stages is expected, something that can be anticipated and viewed as a normal part of a trauma response. Caregivers can also help by supporting care seekers when these returns to earlier stages occur. Care seekers may feel disheartened to discover that the trauma they once thought was in their past is now once again part of their present. They may also feel afraid that this signals an endless return to the trauma or an inability to move beyond it again. Care givers can help by reminding care seekers that what they are experiencing isn't abnormal, shame-filled, or a sign of failure but is rather a natural part of the way humans respond to traumas. They can also help by asking care seekers about the resources that were helpful to them in their initial recovery, as these may be helpful should a relapse occur.

Resolution, therefore, is both possible and cyclical, as evergreen and liminal as trauma itself. The hope for trauma survivors is that the event will eventually become a memory, part of their past rather than a haunting that constitutes their present. In finding ways to build safety, constitute meaning, and reconnect, the survivor has the possibility of moving beyond the trauma and into the future, a future that the caregiver helped to cocreate. A witness to the trauma, the caregiver may now have the honor of becoming a witness to the joy and freedom that lies beyond it. They may have the opportunity to see suffering's transformation and agency's reclamation side by side. Having seen the trauma, they now see the hope that lies beyond it, and may even catch glimpses of the legacy that the care seeker will ultimately leave.

CHAPTER FIVE

Restorative Justice and Trauma-Informed Spiritual Care

Introduction

SPIRITUAL CAREGIVERS CAN call upon many resources to offer effective trauma-informed care. Restorative justice provides one final set of tools that may be a transformative and underutilized resource in this field. Indeed, it is a fitting resource for spiritual caregivers to employ, given the intersection of priorities and practices of each discipline. What follows outlines the philosophy of restorative justice, as well as how that philosophy grounds various practices that can then be utilized in trauma-informed spiritual care.

What is Restorative Justice?

Restorative justice is a philosophy of communication from which a variety of practices emerge, including group conferences, victim-offender mediation, and circle processes. These practices can be utilized both in the aftermath of wrongdoings like traumas as well as in settings where no offense has occurred in order to strengthen community relationships and to promote empathy, agency, and discernment. Restorative processes tend to engage a variety of community members, and many require advanced preparation, as well as the involvement of a facilitator who can lead them. In cases where wrongdoing has occurred, the facilitator should likely also undertake preparation in advance of a process to assess whether various individuals—including the harmed party, the offending party, and the wider community—are capable of participating.

Restorative justice has a long tradition in Indigenous communities and is believed to have originated within them.[1] It has also gained traction in Western cultures and is now the primary justice system in New Zealand for minors as well as a central part of the criminal justice system in Canada. In the United States, twenty states have incorporated restorative justice processes into their justice systems for both minors and adults, including Oregon, Alaska, Pennsylvania, Montana, Nebraska, Arizona, Florida, and West Virginia.[2] In addition, school systems are increasingly turning to restorative practices as an alternative to other forms of accountability—like suspension or expulsion—that are based in punishment rather than meaningful, active accountability.[3]

While restorative justice can be used in any setting, it is perhaps most well-known for providing an alternative to the criminal justice system because it offers an alternative means of accountability. In the United States, for instance, punishment is the *de facto* form of accountability within the criminal justice system. However, there are multiple problems with this system. First, research shows that the punitive philosophy that grounds the criminal justice system is ineffective, especially in comparison to restorative justice.[4] As restorative justice expert Danielle Sered writes in relation to the retributive system in the United States, "If incarceration worked to stop violence, we would have eradicated it by now—because no nation has used incarceration more."[5] Indeed, the United States houses 25 percent of the world's inmates, though it possesses only 5 percent of its population. If this form of accountability were effective, then one would expect the country to have declining rates of violence as well as declining rates of incarceration. Yet this is not the case. According to the United States Sentencing Commission, approximately 65 percent of violent offenders reoffended within two years of being released, as did approximately 40 percent of non-violent offenders.[6]

Additionally, researchers find that punishment effectively instills shame and fear, but it does not encourage positive learning or growth. Put differently, it might teach the offender that they did something wrong, but it fails to teach the offender what the correct alternative is, nor does it make them want to adopt that alternative. In cases where the criminal justice system metes out a prison sentence, punishment also takes a passive rather than an active form. In this passive form, the sheer passage of time becomes synonymous with making things right. It does not, however, require that the wrongdoer reassess their actions, apologize, or take responsibility for what they've done.[7]

Relatedly, psychologists have discovered that the punishment mechanisms at the heart of the criminal justice system rarely facilitate the kind of transformation hoped for in those who commit wrongdoings because punishment, at its best, works by and large according to the tenets of behavioral psychology—it may train someone to be too afraid of negative consequences to such an extent that they no longer engage in behaviors that lead to them (in this case, breaking laws). However, punishment fails to teach an alternative that encourages someone to think and act differently in the world. As a result, people who are punished may wind up avoiding activities that they shouldn't do, but they may not have learned how to live in a healthier way.

The second reason that restorative justice has come to function as an alternative to the criminal justice system is because victim advocates often feel the criminal justice system is both retraumatizing and does not place the needs of victims first. This is partly because the process of working with lawyers and testifying in court can retraumatize victims. It is also because the criminal justice system assigns punishment according to legal codes and not according to what victims feel would be appropriate to make things right.

Finally, studies show that the criminal justice system itself inflicts trauma onto those who find themselves involved in it. Those who enter the criminal justice system are subjected to solitary confinement, sexual violence, bullying, unsanitary living conditions, and a lack of access to medical care.[8] Relatedly, the criminal justice system in the United States is riddled with racial injustice.[9] Statistics show that one in three Black men will be incarcerated during their lifetime, compared to one in six Latinos and one in seventeen whites.[10] Police brutality currently ranks as a leading cause of death among Black men, and a combination of discrimination and mandatory sentencing guidelines ensure that an increasing number of Black individuals will be incarcerated in their lifetimes.[11] As Michelle Alexander argues, "Today's lynching is a felony charge. Today's lynching is incarceration. Today's lynch mobs are criminals. They have a badge; they have a law degree."[12] The insidiousness of racial injustice and trauma within the criminal justice system in the United States makes the system not only ineffective but harmful. It also means that the system does not achieve its stated purpose—which is to make things right for victimized parties and to make the state safer than it was before.

Because restorative justice removes itself from the prison industrial complex, from lawyers, legal codes, and police officers, it seeks to remove itself from the bias inherent in the criminal justice system. This is not to say that restorative justice is immune to racism or to discrimination, largely because racism is embedded in dominant discourses and practitioners are embedded in these as well. However, it is to say that restorative justice is aware of the harm perpetuated by the criminal justice system and, by prioritizing the dignity of every human being—from offending party to victimized party—it seeks to do better.[13]

Restorative practices therefore aim to do exactly what the criminal justice system fails at: They attempt to make things right in the aftermath of wrongdoing by placing the needs of victims front and center. Additionally, they seek to surround the wrongdoer with a system of support, such that they can engage in the challenging work that they need to do to make restitution and change their own lives. Because of these strengths—along with studies showing that restorative practices are more effective at preventing recidivism than punitive approaches are—restorative justice has grown in popularity globally in recent decades.[14]

A final note: Restorative justice has often been criticized for being "light" or for "letting offenders off the hook." This instinct makes sense, given how we collectively assume punishment is the appropriate way to discipline someone who's done something wrong. However, there are several reasons why it's reductive to make these claims about restorative justice. First, restorative justice takes a great deal of time. Prior to any procedure occurring, both the offending parties and victimized parties spend substantial time with facilitators. This work is essential to the success of any process, as it allows the facilitators to understand why the offending party did what they did and also what needs to be done to make things right. Sometimes, this preparatory work can take months.

Second, restorative justice demands introspection. Offending parties have to assess what they've done and then apologize and take steps to make things right, unlike in the criminal justice system, where an offending party could spend years in prison and never have to question the morality of their actions. If offending parties are not capable of this level of introspection, then restorative justice should not be utilized.

Finally, restorative justice recognizes that, at its best, prison has its place. Indeed, some victimized parties would like to see prison time for the offending party as part of the needed restitution. As a result, restorative justice has been used in concert with the criminal justice system when victimized parties feel that a "time out" from society would benefit the offending party or to prevent future harm. For but one example, Andy and Kate Grosmaire engaged in a restorative justice process after their daughter was murdered by her boyfriend, Conor McBride. The couple found the process helpful, because it allowed them to understand why Conor did what he did, and it also gave them a chance to speak freely about the harm that he inflicted upon their family. As part of that process, Andy and Kate nonetheless felt prison time was needed for such a dire offense. They also wanted Conor to have a chance at redemption, which meant they did not want a life sentence. In the end, Conor received twenty years of prison time and ten years of probation. At the request of Andy and Kate, he also agreed to participate in anger management classes, do volunteer work that their daughter had been committed to, and speak publicly about dating violence.

Restorative Justice in Action

A Case Study

Jayden had a car stolen by a teenager named Kendall. How could restorative justice help in such an event? If the case went through the criminal justice system, the state would press charges against Kendall, who might be sent to prison or put on probation. Jayden's opinion on the matter might not be sought out by law enforcement, and Jayden would be left alone to deal with the emotional and practical consequences of the theft.

If Jayden's case relied upon restorative justice, the primacy of relationships and active accountability would look different. In such a case, Jayden's own feelings of what might make things right would guide a way forward. For instance, Jayden would have to want to engage in restorative justice and feel that the process would be meaningful. If that was the case, then Jayden and a facilitator would discern a way forward. If they agreed upon it, the facilitator might convene a circle process, one of the more common manifestations of restorative justice. A **circle process** gathers together the victimized party, offending party, and the wider community affected by the harm together in order to assess the wrongdoing and find effective ways of making things right. Circle processes are, by nature, highly ritualized. Everyone sits in a specific order as designated by the facilitator and is given an opportunity to speak, also in a specific order. A talking piece is often used to designate the speaker; interruptions are not allowed.

Before the process, the facilitator meets with everyone who will be present and asks how the event affected them and what they feel needs to be done to make things right. Wider community members in this scenario include Kendall and Jayden's parents as well as Jayden's spouse. The facilitator would likely ask Kendall about why they committed the crime and whether they understand the nature of the wrong. These questions are designed to help the facilitator assess whether each participant is able to participate in the process. If, for instance, Kendall does not express any kind of remorse for stealing the car, then further conversation would be needed before the circle process can occur, or the process would need to be called off.

Following effective one-on-one conversations, the victimized party (Jayden) and the offending party (Kendall) come together with other members of their community to discuss the wrong and what is needed to make things right, and the circle process begins. Jayden's spouse discusses the trauma she felt after the car was stolen and the stress that the cost of buying a new car places on their relationship. Kendall's parents talk about how disappointed they feel, and Jayden's parents discuss the stress of having to finance a new car for their grown child. Jayden receives a chance to speak directly to Kendall about the wrongdoing and to ask questions that might not get asked in court, including why Kendall chose Jayden's car as opposed to the car parked next door. Jayden also directly tells Kendall what needs to be done to make things right. Kendall agrees to what Jayden asks—namely, to pay for the down payment for a new car. Members of Kendall's community all come up with a plan to support Kendall so that restitution can occur. This includes setting a timeline for saving the money, babysitting Kendall's children so that they can start a second job to get money for the down payment, and actively checking in with Kendall to see how much money has been saved.

There are several benefits to a restorative justice process like this one. First, it is victim-centered, meaning that the process is motivated by the needs of the victimized party. This makes both philosophical and practical sense in cases where wrongdoing has occurred, because it is the victimized party who experiences a lack of agency as a result of the harm. So, when restorative justice places the needs of the harmed party first and allows them to determine what meaningful restitution looks like, it signals that they deserve restored agency and that it is possible. It also signals that there is a community—including the person who enacted the harm and the restorative justice facilitator—who are actively attempting to make that restoration of agency a reality.

Second, restorative justice includes the wider community, thereby recognizing that wrongdoing has two dimensions: It has what chapter 1 described as a horizontal dimension (it impacts not just the person who has been victimized by the offender but also has a rippling effect within the wider community), and it also has a vertical dimension (meaning that wrongs can have an impact across time and between generations). Including the wider community in a restorative response therefore allows members who are part of the vertical and horizontal community affected by the trauma to be included in the process of making things right.

Finally, restorative justice is grounded in relationship, unlike the criminal justice system which offers, as Danielle Sered posits, a passive and objectifying form of accountability.[15] In a courtroom, a judge delivers a sentence to the defendant based upon previously defined minimum sentencing guidelines which the defendant must then carry out, usually by sitting in a prison cell. This is not a relational process, nor is it an active one or a process designed to enhance the subjectivity of the person who committed the wrong.[16] Indeed, the imprisoned party could, theoretically, spend their entire prison sentence never taking accountability for the wrongdoing, never apologizing, never taking steps that the harmed party believes might make things right. In other words, the criminal justice system equates time or minimum sentencing guidelines with accountability rather than encouraging meaningful forms of it. Thus, even if one removed the significant racial bias embedded in the criminal justice system, it remains problematic insofar as it is rooted in forms of accountability that are not meaningful because they are not active or relational.

The Relationship of Restorative Justice to Spiritual Care

It may initially seem as if spiritual caregivers would have little use for restorative justice, since the primary responsibility of such professionals is not to provide an alternative to the criminal justice system. Nonetheless, at a broader scale, both restorative justice practitioners and spiritual caregivers seek to resolve conflict and suffering for the purpose of enabling the flourishing of every human being. In that regard, restorative justice and spiritual care share much in common, both in terms of theory and practice. Case in point: One of the priorities of spiritual care is to place the needs of the most vulnerable first because many care seekers have experienced a violation of agency in the past and benefit from opportunities to regain it in their lives. Indeed, the lack of agency often causes a care seeker to feel vulnerable.[17] Placing the needs of the most vulnerable first, therefore, becomes the priority for caregivers who recognize that the lack of agency and sense of vulnerability that care seekers have contributes to their ongoing distress.[18]

The philosophical commitment to placing the needs of victims first mirrors itself in concrete restorative practices, including empathy, compassion, active listening, self-reflexivity, the use of silence, and the asking of open-ended questions in order to make sure that the caregiver is able to step, momentarily, into the care seeker's shoes.[19] These practices may be used in large-group facilitation or in small group or one-on-one conversations. In each of these settings, facilitators use their skills to empower victimized parties to identify what it would mean to make things right and then help that vision to become a reality. It is not the role of the facilitator to either predetermine an end to a process themselves or try to simply repeat what worked in a previous case. In this way, the role of the facilitator is analogous to that of the spiritual caregiver, who also isn't in the business of problem solving or providing pre-established answers but rather seeks to ask the right questions and do so with the right orientation so that the care seeker can discern the answers for themselves. This distinction matters because it becomes the difference between imposing discernment or meaning onto the care seeker and creating space for the care seeker to do their own work. Establishing opportunities for discernment and the reclaiming of agency is always important in spiritual care. However, as prior chapters establish, it is particularly important when working with traumatized individuals who often feel the event has deprived them of agency.

In addition, restorative justice, like spiritual care, prioritizes issues of power and seeks to address them through its practices. Most obviously, restorative processes address power imbalances and injustices by offering an alternative to a criminal justice system that all too often exploits those who are vulnerable because of the way that the wider society constructed their identity. In this way, restorative justice is not only aware of the current problems with the criminal justice system but is actively seeking to reform them by offering a different way of enacting justice.

Both restorative justice and spiritual care also recognize the value ritual has in facilitating meaning-making, connection, and stability (see chapter 3 for more information on the positive role ritual can play in caregiving). These rituals include—but are not limited to—liturgies from denominational prayerbooks and the public reciting of well-known prayers, as well as rituals developed outside of religious frameworks.[20] Caregivers may also use spontaneous prayer or help a care seeker develop a faith-based ritual that is meaningful to them in order to formally mourn a loss or commemorate a trauma. While faith-based rituals are less common in restorative justice, the use of ritual remains prominent. By way of example, the use of a talking piece and the reliable order of communication in a circle process are simple examples of ritual within restorative practices. In addition, most restorative processes follow a formulaic—or ritualized—framework for what gets covered. Facilitators of circle processes, for instance, usually guide conversation in a particular order following five steps. First, they lead an opening activity that grounds the conversation (i.e., a moment of silence). Then they facilitate an activity designed to build trust among group members that is unrelated to the primary issue at hand (i.e., an ice breaker). Having done that, they transition to leading a discussion about the primary concern, grounded in active listening, "I" statements, empathy, and silence. Next, they guide a discussion in which the group makes decisions about concrete ways to move forward. Finally, they lead a closing ritual or activity (i.e., a closing reflection from each participant).

The reliability of these five stages in a circle process builds trust and safety within the community and functions as a ritual that participants can rely upon, especially if a circle is to be convened more than once. In cases where the circle is being convened to address a trauma, these stages also provide much needed structure and reliability, or, put differently, they reinforce a sense of safety, which survivors of trauma need to heal.[21] These five stages thus attempt to first build trust and safety within the community so that the groundwork is laid for the community to do the important work of meaning-making and reconnection.[22] Significant overlap therefore exists between restorative justice and effective spiritual care, as both view meaning-making and the strengthening of relationships as foundational to the efficacy of their work.

Finally, both restorative justice and spiritual caregiving as fields have a significant interest in intersectionality, which is to say that they both prioritize the importance of naming how intersectional systemic oppression contributes to suffering and how practices of care can be revised to respond to them and prevent further harm.[23] The two fields thus pay significant theoretical attention to issues of race, gender, class, ability, and belief, while also developing concrete practices that can aid in response.[24] While they share this commitment, however, the reasons for doing so are different. Spiritual caregiving as a field emerged from and in conversation with the wisdom of faith traditions that address the dangers of intersectional oppression.[25] The field continues to see these sources as authoritative, meaning they have insights of value for the practice of care. Thus, a commitment to battling intersectional systemic oppression may stem from these faith commitments. In contrast, while restorative justice has been adopted for use in many faith-based communities because its principles align so clearly with them, it is also used widely within secular organizations, and many restorative justice resources make no reference to spirituality or to spiritual practices. As a result, restorative justice's commitment to ending intersectional oppression may be rooted in secular rather than spiritual claims.

More broadly, restorative justice as a field does not necessarily root itself in spirituality in the same way that spiritual caregiving does. In other words, even as there is a significant overlap in core practices between the fields, the theoretical basis for doing so differs.[26] Indeed, many spiritual care practitioners do the work they do because of their faith commitments, and they see the practices of care emerging from them. In contrast, restorative justice in the Western world often emerges from secular claims, namely from the belief that the needs of the most vulnerable deserve priority, especially in the aftermath of a wrongdoing. Having said that, it is also important to recall the history of restorative justice as rooted in Indigenous cultures that place a high value upon spirituality in all aspects of life. As a result, spiritual caregivers who seek to utilize restorative practices should be aware of this history in order to avoid issues of appropriation.

If the reasons for undertaking practices potentially differ, there remains a significant overlap in terms of core practices and beliefs between the fields. Both fields rely heavily upon competencies like active listening and empathy, as well as a desire to enact justice in the world and to place the needs of the most vulnerable first, mindful of the power dynamics that vulnerability creates. Most restorative practices—like the best of spiritual care practices—also give the harmed party a chance to speak freely about their experience of harm to the extent that they're comfortable, as well as the chance to speak freely about what they believe needs to be done to make things right. In this way, the harmed party isn't constrained by legal structures that predetermine the scope of wrongdoing and punishment, thereby taking narrative agency away from the harmed party. Likewise, facilitators of restorative processes take steps before, during, and after processes to ensure that the harmed party's needs come first, just as a spiritual caregiver might do before, during, and after a caregiving conversation.

Restorative Pastoral Caregiving

Restorative processes take several forms, each of which may be potentially useful in the aftermath of trauma. These include not only circle processes but also **victim offender mediation**, a process that allows a victimized party to meet the offending party directly in conversation with a facilitator to have a structured conversation about the harm done and to create a plan for active accountability. A proxy may be used in cases where the victimized party does not want to interact directly with the offending party. Proxies may be neutral parties or they may be offending parties who committed similar wrongdoings.[27] In addition to victim offender mediation, there is also the opportunity to engage in restorative justice for family-related conflicts. For instance, **family group conferences** are structured conversations between family members and a facilitator designed to help families navigate conflict and create a plan for active accountability in cases of wrongdoing. Finally, there are restorative processes for widespread, public harm, notably **truth and reconciliation commissions**. Truth and reconciliation commissions have been used sporadically in cases of national harm, most notably in Canada to address the harm inflicted by its Indian residential school system and in South Africa to address the legacy of apartheid. Rooted in restorative principles, they require wrongdoers to publicly admit to and apologize for the harm done.

Each of these forms of restorative justice, along with circle processes, attempts to place the needs of the most vulnerable first in order to enact active accountability and make things right. In addition, each requires significant preparation and may not be suitable in the aftermath of trauma. Indeed, one of the reasons for such extensive preparation is that it offers the facilitator a chance to discern—along with participants—whether a restorative approach will help to make things right for the injured party. It may be the case that the offending party is unwilling or unable to take accountability for the wrongs done. In such cases, restorative justice may not be the best approach. It may also be the case that a restorative approach is not wanted by the injured party. In this case, it is almost certainly not the right approach. Spiritual caregivers will therefore need to use skills like active listening to determine whether a restorative approach will ultimately help the care seeker reclaim agency, feel safe, make meaning, and reconnect in the aftermath of a trauma.

Conclusion

Restorative justice, like spiritual caregiving, is both a skill and an art. Practitioners must possess core competencies but must also be nimble enough to respond to the needs of the moment to help the most vulnerable regain agency and to make things right for care seekers. While spiritual caregivers often have the skills to do restorative justice work, further training is usually needed to familiarize them with the various techniques and processes involved. These may be learned via short intensive training or long-term training done on a part-time basis. Most can be done in ways that do not disrupt one's current career responsibilities.[28]

While it may take extra training to become familiar with restorative justice principles and processes, the effort may well make a significant difference in the life of a care seeker, especially given the problems in the criminal justice system. Caregivers benefit from the flexibility and freedom that restorative justice has, as it exists apart from legal structures and their constraints. Its emphasis on placing the needs of care seekers first also helps to ensure that justice will be served, where justice is defined as making things right for the harmed party. Spiritual caregivers can help by incorporating these techniques into their practice, thereby giving the benefit afforded by restorative justice to those who seek spiritual restitution and wholeness. Indeed, the significant overlap between the priorities and practices of spiritual care and restorative justice make them natural partners in the effort to lessen the suffering imposed by trauma.

CONCLUSION

The Circular Nature of Trauma and the Signs of Recovery

THE PSYCHOLOGIST MARY Harvey postulates that a person can detect the resolution of trauma after several changes have occurred. First, the survivor feels that the physiological symptoms of the trauma are resolved or are manageable and no longer interfere significantly in their daily life. In addition, the survivor senses that they can tolerate the feelings accompanying the memory of the trauma, and that the memory of the trauma isn't controlling them. Relatedly, the survivor finds that they can structure that memory into a narrative rather than feeling the memory is fragmented, disjointed, and unable to be integrated into their life story. Finally, the survivor feels renewed self-esteem, can participate in meaningful relationships, and possesses a global system of meaning that can hold the story of the trauma without significant conflict.[1]

Spiritual caregivers can assist with alleviating the distress associated with all of these domains, though perhaps it is in regard to the last that they possess the ability to make the most impact. After all, the passion of many spiritual caregivers emerges from a desire to understand how to make sense of the disjunct between those things that seem to be traumatic or evil with hope or belief in a good God. Their unique spiritual traditions offer unique resources, and the core competencies of the field equip them for the task. With their assistance, trauma survivors may be able to find a richer sense of safety that incorporates their spirituality, just as they may be able to resolve global and situational meaning clashes and reestablish how their own sense of self relates to the wider community.

And yet, trauma is both a dot and a circle. As a dot, trauma is a moment in time that seems immovable, that stalls a person or community within it, that keeps them stuck within the event and unable to move beyond it. The inability to see or move within the trauma appears to defy time and makes the trauma appear to be unending. Yet even as trauma seems to be a single point, it is also a circle, because when the recovery process appears to be complete, it is not uncommon for the trauma to return, to rear its head and try to assert its power. In this way, the trauma returns as if cycling back to trap time and the sufferer within it.

The return of trauma can be disheartening to a survivor. And yet, the return of trauma is not the same as its initial appearance, in part because the person has learned so much during the initial recovery journey. Hopefully—with the help of a spiritual caregiver, a therapist, and a supportive community—they have experimented with and found coping mechanisms that work. They may have learned how to seek out support from caregivers, family, and friends. They may have restructured how they understand the trauma itself. They may feel a sense of pride in what they did do to survive. They may also have discovered helpful coping strategies, cultivated grounding practices, found ways to instill holistic safety, and derived meaning. They may have discovered a new sense of self that is affirmed by their community and made meaningful strides in social justice work. In all these ways, they may have inadvertently cultivated resiliency along the recovery journey. This resiliency may not be worth the cost, and yet, it can come in handy when trauma returns. Indeed, spiritual caregivers may want to let caregivers know toward the end of their initial recovery journey that the trauma's effects may return and help them to make a list of coping mechanisms that they can draw on should that happen. In this way, care seekers can be prepared, turning the return of trauma into more of a drizzle than a storm.

One need not live long to see that trauma is ubiquitous, affecting most human lives, instilling sometimes lifelong pain. And yet, hope is just as universal, as is love and goodness and care. Spiritual caregivers, at their best, represents all these things. And while they may not alone solve the problem of trauma in a care seeker's life, they are like a hand extended to a survivor who feels alone and afraid. They are the beginning of a call that says, "I am here. You are not alone. Together, we can find a way through this time, so that you, with the fullness of your story, can step into a new tomorrow."

APPENDIX A

Artistic Suggestions for Trauma Storytelling

Care seekers often need to find ways to tell their stories that allow them to integrate that story into the narrative of their lives. Artistic forms of expression can help with this task, especially when talking about the trauma does not feel comfortable for the care seeker. Below are some examples of artistic forms that care seekers may find helpful as they seek to express the trauma. They have been chosen because they are inexpensive and accessible to individuals who don't have a background in the arts. As a result, care seekers may experience them as less threatening than other art forms, which may also make them feel safer for care seekers.

This list is not intended to be comprehensive but rather to spark the imagination for further ideas for creative endeavors that might be helpful to care seekers. Care seekers may have their own ideas about what might be a helpful way to express and make meaning of their experiences. As always, artistic forms should be feel safe for the care seeker and provide an opportunity to reclaim agency. Please note that these should never be imposed upon care seekers.

Cut-Up (Découpé) Poetry

Poetry can be a helpful form of expression in the aftermath of trauma because of its flexibility and creativity. Many of the established rules of writing can be sacrificed in poetry, which often makes it appeal to trauma survivors because it feels as if it can hold more than prose can. Other trauma survivors, however, may feel intimidated by the idea of writing a poem. Does it have to rhyme? Isn't it supposed to have a certain rhythm? Or will it just sound childish?

One way to make poetry accessible is to offer care seekers the opportunity to write a cut-up poem, also known as a *découpé* poem. To write a cut-up poem, the caregiver provides a set of words to the care seeker. Caregivers can use the magnetic sets that people use on their refrigerators; alternatively, they can provide non-triggering internet or magazine articles for reference. The care seeker then chooses from among the words provided and rearranges them into any order of their choosing. After they've completed the composition, the care seeker may choose to share it with the caregiver and discuss the process of writing the poem as well as what the poem means to them.

Collage

Collage might be considered the visual art equivalent to cut-up poetry. As with cut-up poetry, it doesn't require creating the building blocks for the art form. Instead, care seekers receive these in advance and use them to create their own new art form. Caregivers may want to consider providing care seekers with images from magazines or pre-existing images of art forms that they can then glue together in whatever design they see fit. After creating the image, care seekers can decide whether to share it with others, including the caregiver. If it feels safe to them, they can share what the process of creating the image was like, as well as how they interpret the meaning of the image they created.

Journaling

There are several reasons why journaling can be a helpful resource for trauma survivors. First, it is an activity over which care seekers have total control—they can write when they want, can erase or cross out the words or stories that don't fit what they want to say, and they can write when and where they choose. In other words, journaling gives trauma survivors a chance to craft a narrative of how the event affected their lives and to do so in a way that gives them control over the story.

One of the other benefits of journaling is that it is an activity that takes place over time. Because it is ongoing, care seekers can track their story's development, including how their feelings, memories, and embodied reactions to the trauma change over time. It also gives them a chance to process clashes between their global and situational meaning-making capacities, to state where those clashes are and to explore ways to resolve them. The privacy of journaling can be particularly helpful for trauma survivors as they navigate these clashes, as they do not have to worry about how what they write might be received by a listener—the writing only exists for them. In this way, journaling gives a care seeker control over what they choose to say and how they choose to say it in a way that is non-threatening, thereby holding the potential to dissipate shame and suffering.

Making a Music Playlist

One of the purposes of music is to communicate that which seems to be beyond words alone. By incorporating sound, in all its multiplicity, music is expansive, creative, and manages to capture the joy, wonder, fear, hopelessness, and hope of human existence. Music also involves the whole body, as sound vibrates in the body, in the tiny parts of the inner ear, the sinuses, the skin. Yet even as music involves the whole body, it does so safely, without one body touching another. The care seeker can always turn it off, switch to another tune. Music can also provide a way for care seekers to feel a sense of connection or solidarity, the recognition that someone beyond them has experiences that, in some way, resonate with theirs. That feeling of being understood can thereby provide survivors with an antidote to the isolation that frequently accompanies trauma.

Creating a playlist can be a resource for trauma survivors who find meaning and comfort in music but who—for any number of reasons—do not want to create music from scratch on their own. Playlists can be created using apps like Spotify or Apple Music, and they can even be written on a piece of paper. They may be shared with trusted others, like caregivers, or listened to in privacy. If they are shared with the caregiver, the care seeker may want to explain why they chose the pieces they did, why they put pieces in a particular order, and why the songs are meaningful to them.

APPENDIX B

Global and Situational Meaning Clashes

MEANING CLASHES CAN occur when there is a difference in one's global meaning and the meaning one assigned to a specific event (situational meaning). The chart below illustrates how this clash occurs and can be resolved.

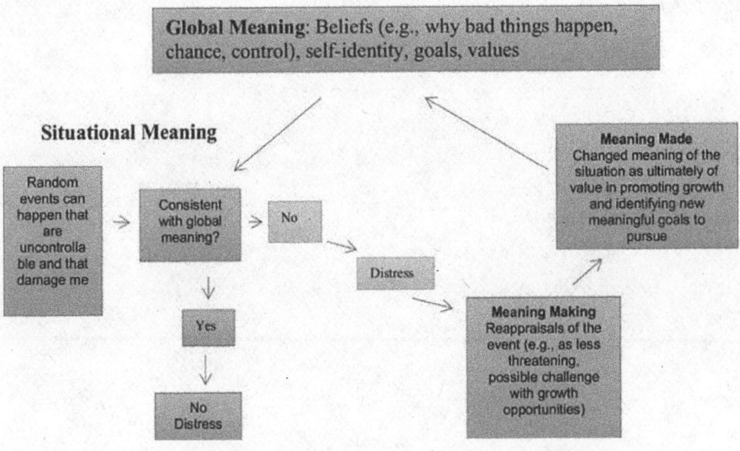

Reprinted from Park, "Meaning-Making Following Trauma."

APPENDIX C

FICA Screening Tool

THE FICA IS a short spiritual screening tool rooted in the acronym that makes up its title. It is composed of questions related to four areas of a person's spiritual life and helps caregivers to assess a person's spiritual background, as well as their embedded beliefs, clashes in meaning, and current support system and resources.

F (Faith and Belief): "Do you consider yourself spiritual or religious?" or "Do you have spiritual beliefs that help you cope with stress?"

I (Importance): "What importance does your faith or belief have in our life? Have your beliefs influenced how you take care of yourself in this illness?"

C (Community): "Are you part of a spiritual or religious community? Is this of support to you and how?"

A (Address in Care): "How would you like me, your spiritual care provider, to address these issues in your care?"

Adapted from C.M. Puchaflski and A.L. Romer, "Taking a Spiritual History allows Clinicians to Understand Patients More Fully. *Journal of Palliative Medicine* 3, no. 1 (2000):129–137.

GLOSSARY

active listening The act of giving full attention to what a care seeker says.

acute stress response See "fight, flight, or freeze response."

adrenaline A hormone and neurotransmitter manufactured by the adrenal gland. It causes a rise in heart rate, blood circulation, and breathing, and increases the amount of blood sent to the body's brain and muscles. It also increases alertness and blood pressure. Adrenaline is a key factor in the body's fight, fight, or freeze response (see "fight, flight, or freeze response").

amygdala The part of the brain that activates the body's stress response; it can become overactive when reminded of the trauma. Heightened levels cause physiological arousal as well as increased heart rate, oxygen levels, and blood pressure.

anxious attachment An attachment style that emerges when children only receive sporadic support from caregivers. Caregivers are therefore seen as unreliable, and children's emotional or physical needs may not be met. Adults who grew up with this attachment style often have a hard time trusting others and developing close relationships and may be clingy or distrustful in they see others as fundamentally untrustworthy.

arousal symptoms A set of symptoms commonly experienced as part of the PTSD symptom cluster. Difficulty sleeping, irrational outbursts of anger, aggression, heightened startle response, feelings of shame, and self-destructive acts are all considered arousal symptoms.

attachment style A psychological theory that holds that children's relationship with caregivers impacts their social-emotional development and future relationships. Early attachment often predicts later attachment styles. Cultural factors can affect attachment style. See "secure attachment," "insecure attachment," "anxious attachment," "avoidant attachment" and "disorganized attachment" for more details.

avoidance symptoms A cluster of PTSD symptoms in which a person consciously or unconsciously tries to avoid cues related to the trauma. These include emotional numbing, and attempts to avoid talking about, thinking about, remembering, or visiting the site of the trauma.

avoidant attachment An attachment style that emerges when caregivers demean or reject children. It may also occur when the child is placed into a caregiving role for the parent. Children exposed to this form of caregiving often decide it is best to keep a distance from the caregiver, thereby emphasizing self-reliance and avoidance of their own emotions. Adults with an avoidant attachment style may struggle with intimacy or to develop close relationships with others.

Auden's Rule The idea that a care seeker does not need to know all the details of a trauma to help a care seeker. Instead, they need to create the conditions for a care seeker to share what they need to share in order to alleviate their distress.

Broca's area A part of the brain responsible for language. It may be inhibited in the aftermath of a trauma, making speech production difficult.

circle process A type of restorative justice process that gathers together the victimized party, offending party, and community members in a circle with a facilitator. Conversation is structured around making things right for the victimized party. Usually, the facilitator does preparatory work with all parties, and a talking piece is used to ensure ordered communication.

The Church of Jesus Christ of Latter-Day Saints A Christian denomination founded by Joseph Smith in upstate New York in the 1800s. Smith reported receiving a set of golden plates from an angel named Moroni which contained a text that Smith dictated. The contents of the plates became known as the Book of Mormon. Members consider the Book of Mormon to have the same authority as the Old and New Testaments of the Bible.

disorganized attachment A style of attachment that develops when a child has a caregiver who frightens or hurts them. Children may eventually respond to the caregiver by fighting back or becoming self-reliant. Caregivers often have a history of unresolved trauma, and without support, teenagers exposed to this form of attachment with a caregiver exhibit higher than normal levels of psychopathology.[1]

DSM Stands for *The Diagnostic and Statistical Manual of Mental Disorders*. This book provides the diagnostic criteria for various mental health disorders.

deliberative beliefs Intentionally chosen beliefs that may or may not align with previously held embedded beliefs.

embedded beliefs Beliefs that one inherits about global meaning that are usually unexamined and assumed to be true.

emotional flooding A feeling that one is being overwhelmed by intense and uncontrollable feelings.

etiological event The event that causes PTSD symptoms to emerge, also known as an "originating event."

family group conference A restorative justice practice in which family members and a facilitator engage in a structured conversation to resolve conflict and create a plan for active accountability in cases of wrongdoing.

felt sense of safety A feeling that one is safe. This differs from quantifiable safety (i.e., that one has a house or clothes) and instead relates to the sense of safety that one feels in one's own body.

fight, flight, or freeze response These are three ways of responding to an acute stressor. The fight response encompasses physical signs like kicking, hitting, crying, verbally reasoning, or preparing to fight. The flight response also involves physical movement, including running. The freeze response happens when a person is unable to move or respond during a potentially traumatic event. All three may be ways of responding to the potentially traumatic event.

Fundamentalist Church of Jesus Christ of Latter-Day Saints (FLDS) A religious group—widely labeled as a "sect" or "cult"—that practices polygamy and isolates members from the outside world. The group does not bear a current relationship to the Church of Jesus Christ of Latter-Day Saints (also colloquially referred to as the "Mormon Church"), although both place great value on founder Joseph Smith's revelations.

gift of silence The skill of recognizing that silence can be helpful in spiritual care conversations and the ability to use it well.

global meaning A person's overall worldview or the way they make sense of the world at large.

hermeneutic of belief The act of assuming belief in a care seeker's story.

insecure attachment A form of attachment style that tends to emerge when a primary caregiver fails to meet the emotional, psychological, or physical needs of a child. Insecure attachment styles may vary. See "anxious attachment," "avoidant attachment," and "disorganized attachment" for the forms that insecure attachment takes.

integration The process of taking parts of a person's story or identity that do not seem to make sense in light of other parts of their story or identity and resolving them in a way that feels meaningful, cohesive, and that eliminates distress.

intrusive symptoms A cluster of PTSD symptoms in which individuals receive unwanted reminders of the trauma. These may include flashbacks, unwanted memories, nightmares, and conscious or unconscious reenactments of the trauma.

intergenerational trauma A trauma whose effects transmit across generations. These effects may be subtle or profound, and individuals may or may not be consciously aware of their relationship to the original trauma.

liminal space A transitional space or a space not meant to be permanently inhabited.

mandated reporter A person required to report abuse to legal authorities. Mandated reporters are usually required to report abuse of vulnerable parties (i.e., the elderly, children, and those with disabilities) to government officials within a specific time. Spiritual care providers are often considered mandated reporters.

meaning-making clash Discomfort that arises due to dissonances between the meaning one initially attributes to a given situation (situational meaning) and the meaning previously derived about their worldview (global meaning). To alleviate the discomfort, the suffering party must find a way to resolve the places where global and situational meaning clash against one another. This can be done by modifying the meaning attributed to the situation, modifying one's global meaning, or both.

moral injury Distress that emerges after a person participates in, cannot prevent, or observes an event that violates their moral compass.

Mormon A member of The Church of Jesus Christ of Latter-Day Saints. See also "The Church of Jesus Christ of Latter-Day Saints."

post-traumatic growth Psychological or spiritual growth or learning that occurs in the aftermath of a trauma.

post-traumatic stress disorder (PTSD) A psychological diagnosis that can be made in the aftermath of a potentially traumatic event if a person experiences significant psychological distress. Symptoms include avoidance, intrusive, and arousal symptoms. Individuals with PTSD may also be concurrently diagnosed with other disorders, notably those related to depression and anxiety. See "intrusive symptoms," "arousal symptoms," and "avoidance symptoms."

reasonable confidentiality The expectation that a caregiver will not repeat the contents of a caregiving conversation, unless the care seeker is planning to hurt themselves or others, or the care seeker has been a victim of abuse that must be reported to the government.

resiliency Skills that allow a person to adapt after a trauma. A person may possess such skills prior to the trauma occurring.

secondary trauma The indirect experience of a potentially traumatic event that gets processed as a trauma by an individual, group, or community.

secure attachment An attachment style in which caregivers offer children freedom to explore while being emotionally and physically available to support children as needed. Adults who grow up with this attachment history are more likely to have healthy self-esteem, emotional awareness, and relationships with others.

self-differentiation The ability to see one's self as different from others. Self-differentiation involves an awareness of one's own biases, an openness to ideas that differ from one's own, and an ability to tolerate difference and complexity.

self-reflexivity The capacity to reflect on one's self, including one's background, family, assumptions, and beliefs.

situational meaning The meaning or purpose attributed to a given situation.

spiritual processing The act of changing memory structures related to one's global worldview in order to change the interpretative meaning and physiological response given to an event.

stress An event or ongoing series of events that taxes a person's coping mechanisms, making them feel that they cannot meet the demands of their environment, but not to the point that their coping mechanisms are overwhelmed.

trauma A highly distressing event or series of events that occurs in the life of an individual or community, which overwhelms their capacity to cope, often because of a sense of threat to their lives and what is most meaningful to them.

truth and reconciliation commission A restorative justice practice in which wrongdoers publicly admit to and apologize for the harms they enacted. Truth and reconciliation commissions are most often used in cases of widespread harm, notably in South Africa after apartheid.

unconditional positive regard The act of a caregiver offering complete acceptance and support for a care seeker simply because they are the care seeker and not because of anything they do or say.

victim offender mediation A restorative justice practice in which victimized parties speak directly with the offending party in conversation with a facilitator to have a structured conversation about the harm done and to create a plan for active accountability. Proxies can be utilized when victimized parties do not want to interact directly with offending parties.

NOTES

PREFACE

1. For a book length discussion of how pastoral theology as a field can respond to the problems posed by theodicy, see John Swinton, *Raging with Compassion: Pastoral Responses to the Problem of Evil* (Grand Rapids, MI: Eerdmans, 2007). For two book length philosophy of religion treatises that explicitly attempt to respond to the question of how God can make mortal life good on the whole in light of the existence of evil, see Marilyn McCord Adams, *Horrendous Evils and the Goodness of God*, (Ithaca: Cornell University Press, 2000); Marilyn McCord Adams, *Christ and Horrors: The Coherence of Christology*, (New York: Cambridge University Press, 2006).

INTRODUCTION

1. The authors state that they utilized the composite international diagnostic interview (CIDI) to see whether individuals had been exposed to any of the criteria listed in Criterion A1 for PTSD. They referred to the list as "traumatic events," although this is something of a misnomer, as the list of events in Criterion A1 are not in and of themselves traumatic but rather are considered by the psychological community to be the kind of events that might elicit a PTSD response. It should be noted that there is a long history of debating what events should be included in the A1 Criterion. For an in-depth analysis of the history of that criterion, see Danielle Tumminio Hansen, *Speaking of Rape: The Limits of Language in Sexual Violations* (Minneapolis: Fortress Press, 2024). For more information on the "traumatic events" listed in the study, see C. Benjet et al., "The Epidemiology of Traumatic Event Exposure Worldwide: Results from the World Mental Health Survey Consortium," *Psychological Medicine* 46, no. 2 (January 2016): 327–343, https://doi.org/10.1017/S0033291715001981.

2. Benjet et al., "The Epidemiology of Traumatic Event Exposure Worldwide."
3. Melissa T. Merrick, "Vital Signs: Estimated Proportion of Adult Health Problems Attributable to Adverse Childhood Experiences and Implications for Prevention—25 States, 2015–2017," *MMWR. Morbidity and Mortality Weekly Report* 68 (2019), https://doi.org/10.15585/mmwr.mm6844e1.
4. For a paradigmatic introduction to core competencies in pastoral care, see Carrie Doehring, *The Practice of Pastoral Care: A Postmodern Approach*, revised and expanded edition (Louisville, KY: Westminster John Knox Press, 2015). For a summary of core competencies, specifically in relation to spiritual care and chaplaincy, see part 3 of Shelly Rambo and Wendy Cadge's *Chaplaincy and Spiritual Care in the Twenty-First Century* (Chapel Hill: University of North Carolina Press, 2022), 129–192.
5. I've written about this part of my life and the theoretical issues that emerged from my experiences extensively in Tumminio Hansen, *Speaking of Rape*.

CHAPTER ONE

1. For a helpful primer on the distinctions between stress, crisis, and trauma, see Catherine N. Dulmus and Carolyn Hilarski, "When Stress Constitutes Trauma and Trauma Constitutes Crisis: The Stress-Trauma-Crisis Continuum," *Brief Treatment and Crisis Intervention* 3, no. 1 (2003): 27–35, https://doi.org/10.1093/brief-treatment/mhg008.
2. Judith Herman, *Trauma and Recovery: The Aftermath of Violence—from Domestic Abuse to Political Terror* (New York: Basic Books, 1997), 33.
3. Resiliency as a concept has often been used to construct Black women's identity as inviolable. Drawing on the work of Emilie Townes, Stephanie Crumpton observes that, "While cultural selfobjects certainly show up in culturally produced stereotypes emerging out of other groups to depict Black women as loud-mouthed (the Sapphire) and self-sacrificing (the Mammy), some of these cultural selfobjects emerge out of the African American community's own 'self' as a result of its intragroup struggles with colorism, sexism, classism, and homophobia. In these instances, the psychological stakes are higher for Black girls and women who encounter language as a cultural selfobject present in the conversations that they have with members of their own communities. One such example is language in which words like 'strong' are used to laud Black women's resilience, without acknowledging the dehumanizing way in

which this descriptor portrays them as invincible in the face of death-dealing circumstances." Stephanie M. Crumpton, *A Womanist Pastoral Theology Against Intimate and Cultural Violence* (Palgrave Macmillan, 2014), 15–6.

4. Pargament and Exline, *Working with Spiritual Struggles in Psychotherapy*.
5. Bessel van der Kolk, *The Body Keeps the Score: Brain, Mind, and Body in the Healing of Trauma* (New York: Viking, 2014), 46.
6. Van der Kolk, *The Body Keeps the Score*, 43–45.
7. Van der Kolk, *The Body Keeps the Score*, 44–45.
8. Chanel Miller, *Know My Name* (New York: Penguin Random House, 2019), 9.
9. For a more expanded consideration of desire as it relates to our theological anthropology and construction of the self, see Danielle Tumminio Hansen, *Conceiving Family: A Practical Theology of Surrogacy and Self* (Waco, TX: Baylor University Press, 2019), 13–17.
10. For a book-length exploration of multiple meanings of the term "hope" and how spiritual caregivers and care seekers benefit from understanding them, see Pamela R. McCarroll, *The End of Hope—The Beginning: Narratives of Hope in the Face of Death and Trauma* (Minneapolis: Fortress Press, 2014).
11. Carrie Doehring, *The Practice of Pastoral Care: A Postmodern Approach*, revised and expanded edition (Louisville, KY: Westminster John Knox Press, 2015), 13.
12. As Carmen Maria Machado writes in a fictional story in which a woman is raped and impregnated: "If this child is part of The Plan, then The Plan was that I would be raped. If this child is not part of The Plan, then my rape was a violation of The Plan, in which case The Plan is not a Plan at all, but a Polite fucking Suggestion." Carmen Maria Machado, *Her Body and Other Parties* (Minneapolis: Graywolf Press, 2017), 98.
13. For more on religious coping strategies and resources for those suffering from spiritual struggles, see Kenneth I. Pargament, *The Psychology of Religion and Coping: Theory, Research, Practice* (New York: The Guilford Press, 2001). See also Pargament and Exline, *Working with Spiritual Struggles in Psychotherapy*.
14. Peter Loewenberg, "Clinical and Historical Perspectives on the Intergenerational Transmission of Trauma," in *Lost in Transmission: Studies of Trauma Across Generations*, ed. M. Gerard Fromm (London: Routledge, 2012), 61.
15. Loewenberg, "Clinical and Historical Perspectives on the Intergenerational Transmission of Trauma," 61–62.

16. Brett Kavanaugh, quoted in Lawrence Hurley, "U.S. Supreme Court Expands State Power over Native American Tribes," *Reuters*, June 30, 2022, sec. United States, https://www.reuters.com/world/us/us-supreme-court-expands-state-power-over-tribes-win-oklahoma-2022-06-29/.
17. M. Gerard Fromm, *Lost in Transmission: Studies of Trauma Across Generations* (London: Routledge, 2012), xxi.
18. US Department of Health and Human Services, "Understanding Child Trauma," accessed January 24, 2023, https://www.samhsa.gov/child-trauma/understanding-child-trauma.
19. CDC, "Fast Fact: Preventing School Violence," September 2, 2021, https://www.cdc.gov/violenceprevention/youthviolence/schoolviolence/fastfact.html.
20. CDC, "Fast Facts: Preventing Child Abuse & Neglect," April 6, 2022, https://www.cdc.gov/violenceprevention/childabuseandneglect/fastfact.html.
21. We see this tendency in adults as well in cases of Stockholm syndrome.
22. Van der Kolk, *The Body Keeps the Score*, 133–135.
23. Matthew C. Fadus, et al., "Unconscious Bias and the Diagnosis of Disruptive Behavior Disorders and ADHD in African American and Hispanic Youth," *Academic Psychiatry* 44, no. 1 (February 1, 2020): 95–102, https://doi.org/10.1007/s40596-019-01127-6.
24. Harvard Medical School, "National Comorbidity Survey," 2005, https://www.hcp.med.harvard.edu/ncs/index.php.
25. Paula P. Schnurr, "Epidemiology and Impact of PTSD," PTSD: National Center for PTSD, US Department of Veteran Affairs, accessed January 23, 2023, https://www.ptsd.va.gov/professional/treat/essentials/epidemiology.asp.
26. Emily J. Ozer et al., "Predictors of Posttraumatic Stress Disorder and Symptoms in Adults: A Meta-Analysis," *Psychological Bulletin* 129, no. 1 (January 2003): 52–73, https://doi.org/10.1037/0033-2909.129.1.52.
27. Anushka R. Patel and Brian J. Hall, "Beyond the DSM-5 Diagnoses: A Cross-Cultural Approach to Assessing Trauma Reactions," *FOCUS* 19, no. 2 (June 2021): 197–203, https://doi.org/10.1176/appi.focus.20200049.
28. Herman, *Trauma and Recovery*, 237.
29. Osofsky, J.D., Putnam, F.W., & Lederman, C. (2008). "How to Maintain Emotional Health When Working with Trauma. *Juvenile and Family Court Journal*, 59(4), 91–102. Figley, C. (1995). *Compassion Fatigue: Coping with Secondary Traumatic Stress Disorder in Those*

Who Treat the Traumatized (New York: Brunner-Routledge, 1995), 1433–1441.

30. For a more detailed description of core competencies in spiritual care, including self-reflexivity and self-differentiation, see Carrie Doehring and Allison Kestenbaum, "Interpersonal Competencies for Cultivating Spiritual Trust," in *Chaplaincy and Spiritual Care in the Twenty-First Century*, eds. Wendy Cadge and Shelly Rambo (Chapel Hill: University of North Carolina Press, 2022), 134–155.
31. Bessel A. van der Kolk et al., "Yoga as an Adjunctive Treatment for Posttraumatic Stress Disorder: A Randomized Controlled Trial," *Journal of Clinical Psychiatry* 75, no. 6 (June 15, 2014): e559–565, https://doi.org/10.4088/JCP.13m08561.

CHAPTER TWO

1. Kenneth I. Pargament and Julie J. Exline, *Working with Spiritual Struggles in Psychotherapy: From Research to Practice* (New York: The Guilford Press, 2021).
2. Caregivers who are unfamiliar with suicide assessment can benefit from training to administer the Columbia Suicide Severity Rating Scale (C-SSRS). No prior mental health training is needed to learn to administer this short questionnaire, which asks questions related to suicidal ideation in order to assess the risk that a person may take their own life.
3. Discrimination of non-white individuals throughout the criminal justice system can make calling 911 a tenuous enterprise, especially if there is a concern that police may be sent instead of medical professionals. Some caregivers prefer to avoid calling 911 for this reason. There is no easy solution for individuals who are navigating precarious systems that can do harm. Caregivers need to be aware of the risks as well as the benefits of calling for emergency assistance, and an awareness of various resources in their community may help them to avoid calling a resource that will enact concrete harm rather than concrete help.
4. For more on the distinction between secrecy and privacy, see Emma J. Justes, *Please Don't Tell: What to Do with the Secrets People Share*, (Nashville: Abingdon Press, 2014), 41–55.
5. For more on psychological safety in regard to esteem and respect, see Timothy R. Clark, *The 4 Stages of Psychological Safety: Defining the Path to Inclusion and Innovation*, (Oakland, CA: Berrett-Koehler Publishers, 2020). To learn more about psychological safety as a space

for free expression, see William A. Kahn, "Psychological Conditions of Personal Engagement and Disengagement at Work," *Academy of Management Journal* 33, no. 4 (1990): 692–724.

6. These laws vary both internationally and by state in the United States. Readers should check their local jurisdiction to understand what the limits of confidentiality are in spiritual caregiving relationships.
7. The Pew Forum routinely surveys the landscape of American religion and has reported on the rise of the "Nones" and the "spiritual but not religious" cohorts of Americans over time. For a summary of recent research, see Gregory A. Smith, "About Three-in-Ten U.S. Adults Are Now Religiously Unaffiliated," *Pew Research Center's Religion & Public Life Project* (blog), December 14, 2021, https://www.pewresearch.org/religion/2021/12/14/about-three-in-ten-u-s-adults-are-now-religiously-unaffiliated/.
8. Danjuma Gibson challenges some of this research when he proposes that many trauma survivors already know that God loves them; however, that knowledge alone is not enough to counter the reality of PTSD symptoms. He suggests that sometimes faith leaders use platitudes as a way to provide answers and gloss over the real suffering of trauma survivors in ways that reinforce theologies of Christian triumphalism rather than putting the needs of care seekers first and recognizing they are doing the best they can to survive the effects of the trauma. Danjuma Gibson, "Christian Triumphalism: The Antithesis to Trauma Recovery," *FORUM: Calvin Seminary Forum* 27, no. 2 (Winter 2020).
9. Pargament, *The Psychology of Religion and Coping*; Kenneth I. Pargament, ed., *APA Handbook of Psychology, Religion, and Spirituality* (Washington, DC: American Psychological Association, 2013); Kenneth Pargament, Margaret Feuille, and Donna Burdzy, "The Brief RCOPE: Current Psychometric Status of a Short Measure of Religious Coping," *Religions* 2, no. 1 (March 2011): 51–76, https://doi.org/10.3390/rel2010051.
10. Kenneth I. Pargament et al., "Religious Coping Methods as Predictors of Psychological, Physical and Spiritual Outcomes among Medically Ill Elderly Patients: A Two-Year Longitudinal Study," *Journal of Health Psychology* 9, no. 6 (November 2004): 713–730, https://doi.org/10.1177/1359105304045366.
11. "Fundamentalist Church of Jesus Christ of Latter-Day Saints," Southern Poverty Law Center, accessed February 11, 2023, https://www.splcenter.org/fighting-hate/extremist-files/group/fundamentalist-church-jesus-christ-latter-day-saints.

12. For a powerful primer on the FLDS that incorporates accounts of trauma and their spiritual implications by former members, see the docuseries *Keep Sweet: Pray and Obey* (Netflix, 2022).
13. Smart has also publicly challenged the Mormon Church, particularly around issues related to purity culture.
14. For a selection of ground-breaking essays on pastoral care with survivors of sexual violations, see Pamela Cooper-White, *Gender, Violence, and Justice: Collected Essays on Violence against Women* (Cascade Books, 2019).
15. For a more in-depth analysis of both stereotypes about sexual violations and the importance of employing a hermeneutic of belief in spiritual care with survivors, see chapters 2 and 5 of Kristen J. Leslie, *When Violence Is No Stranger: Pastoral Counseling with Survivors of Acquaintance Rape* (Minneapolis: Fortress Press, 2002).
16. For an important introduction to listening practices, see Emma J. Justes, *Hearing Beyond the Words: How to Become a Listening Pastor* (Nashville: Abingdon Press, 2002).
17. Van der Kolk, *The Body Keeps the Score*, 125.
18. "New Year Letter," W. H. Auden, *Collected Poems of W. H. Auden* (New York: Vintage, 1991), 206.
19. See Brian Arao and Kristi Clemens, "From Safe Spaces to Brave Spaces" in *The Art of Effective Facilitation: Reflections From Social Justice Educators*, ed. Lisa M. Landreman (Sterling, VA: Stylus Publishing, 2013), 135–151.
20. Bruce Rogers-Vaughn observes that economic structures in the United States contribute to spiritual suffering, particularly in regard to the way that neoliberalism has infiltrated how people experience their own identity. He observes that the individualism embedded in neoliberalism leads to the conclusion that suffering emerges from individual choices, thereby overlooking the role that structural forces play in causing and perpetuating suffering. As a result, individuals suffer more because they feel a greater sense of personal responsibility than they should for the wrongs they must encounter and respond to. For a book-length consideration of the topic, see Bruce Rogers-Vaughn, *Caring for Souls in a Neoliberal Age* (New York: Palgrave Macmillan, 2016).

CHAPTER THREE

1. Here I use the term "spiritually process" as an extension of the term "emotionally process," which mental health clinicians use as a way of describing changes to memory structures that can change

the interpretative meaning given to an event and the physiological response that accompanies it. Whereas emotional processing refers to changes that affect the emotion attributed to the event, spiritual processing incorporates meaning related to one's worldview. For more on emotional processing, see E. B. Foa and S. P. Cahill, "Psychological Therapies: Emotional Processing," in *International Encyclopedia of the Social & Behavioral Sciences*, ed. Neil J. Smelser and Paul B. Baltes (Oxford: Pergamon, 2001), 12363–69; Wiljo J.P.J. van Hout and Paul M.G. Emmelkamp, "Exposure in Vivo Therapy," in *Encyclopedia of Psychotherapy*, ed. Michael Hersen and William Sledge (Cambridge, MA: Academic Press, 2002), 761–768.

2. The authors conclude that, "The results indicated that emotional (anger, death anxiety), social (social isolation), behavioral (smoking status), and spiritual (insecure relationship with God) burdens moderated the relationship between stressful life events and R/S struggle. Cognitive (self-esteem, optimism), social (emotional support), and spiritual (religious hope) resources did not moderate this relationship." Kelly M. Trevino et al., "Stressful Events and Religious/Spiritual Struggle: Moderating Effects of the General Orienting System," *Psychology of Religion and Spirituality* 11 (2019): 214–224, https://doi.org/10.1037/rel0000149.
3. Crystal L. Park and Ian A. Gutierrez, "Global and Situational Meanings in the Context of Trauma: Relations with Psychological Well-Being," *Counselling Psychology Quarterly* 26, no. 1 (March 1, 2013): 8–25, https://doi.org/10.1080/09515070.2012.727547.
4. Crystal L. Park, "Meaning-Making Following Trauma," *Frontiers in Psychology* 13 (March 23, 2022): 844–891, https://doi.org/10.3389/fpsyg.2022.844891; Crystal L. Park, "Making Sense of the Meaning Literature: An Integrative Review of Meaning-Making and Its Effects on Adjustment to Stressful Life Events," *Psychological Bulletin* 136, no. 2 (March 2010): 257–301, https://doi.org/10.1037/a0018301; Crystal L. Park, "Distinctions to Promote an Integrated Perspective on Meaning: Global Meaning and Meaning-Making Processes," *Journal of Constructivist Psychology* 30, no. 1 (January 2, 2017): 14–19, https://doi.org/10.1080/10720537.2015.1119082.
5. Lily A. Brown et al., "A Review of the Role of Negative Cognitions about Oneself, Others, and the World in the Treatment of PTSD," *Cognitive Therapy and Research* 43, no. 1 (February 1, 2019): 143–173, https://doi.org/10.1007/s10608-018-9938-1.

6. Crystal L. Park et al., "Assessing Disruptions in Meaning: Development of the Global Meaning Violation Scale," *Cognitive Therapy and Research* 40, no. 6 (December 1, 2016): 831–846, https://doi.org/10.1007/s10608-016-9794-9.
7. Doehring, *The Practice of Pastoral Care,* 18–25.
8. Doehring, *The Practice of Pastoral Care,* 18–25.
9. Doehring, *The Practice of Pastoral Care,* 18–25.
10. For more on liberative spiritual integration as derived from Herman's threefold model of healing from trauma, see Doehring, *The Practice of Pastoral Care,* 173–186.
11. Park, "Meaning-Making Following Trauma."
12. Susan J. Brison, *Aftermath* (Princeton: Princeton University Press, 2003), xi.
13. For an important multidisciplinary analysis of testimony in trauma, see Dori Laub and Shoshana Felman, *Testimony: Crises of Witnessing in Literature, Psychoanalysis and History* (London: Routledge, 1991).
14. For a book-length treatment of the importance and practicalities of spiritual assessment, see George Fitchett, *Assessing Spiritual Needs* (Academic Renewal Press, 2002).
15. For an extended analysis of how ritual can be used as a resource in spiritual care, see Rochelle Robins and Danielle Tumminio Hansen, "Meaning-Making through Ritual and Public Leadership," in *Chaplaincy and Spiritual Care in the Twenty-First Century: An Introduction* (Chapel Hill: University of North Carolina Press, 2022), 110–125.
16. Agger and Jensen note that testimony may function as a kind of ritual. See Inger Agger and Søren Buus Jensen, "Testimony as Ritual and Evidence in Psychotherapy for Political Refugees," *Journal of Traumatic Stress* 3, no. 1 (1990): 115–130.
17. Robins and Tumminio Hansen, 110–125.
18. Robins and Tumminio Hansen, 114–115.
19. For a book length exploration of spiritual care resources related to moral injury in military contexts, see Nancy Ramsay and Carrie Doehring, eds., *Military Moral Injury and Spiritual Care: A Resource for Religious Leaders and Professional Caregivers* (Chalice Press, 2019). Wisdom from this work can also be extrapolated to other situations in which moral injury occurred.
20. Tori DeAngelis, "The Legacy of Trauma: An Emerging Line of Research Is Exploring How Historical and Cultural Trauma Affect Survivors'

Children for Generations to Come," *American Psychological Association Monitor* 5, no. 2 (July 3, 2019): 36.

21. Susan J. Brison, *Aftermath: Violence and the Remaking of a Self* (Princeton, NJ: Princeton University Press, 2002), 11.
22. For a critique of this tradition, see Kate Bowler, *Everything Happens for a Reason: And Other Lies I've Loved*, (New York: Random House Trade Paperbacks, 2019).
23. This use of power might be described as the exercise of agential power (power that guides and influences) rather than receptive power (power that takes in and receives). For more on these distinctions in forms of power that a caregiver can utilize, see Doehring, *The Practice of Pastoral Care*, 45.
24. For a book length exploration of how the limits of language affect the processing of trauma and the act of supporting survivors, see Tumminio Hansen, *Speaking of Rape: The Limits of Language in Sexual Violations.*

CHAPTER FOUR

1. Herman, *Trauma and Recovery*, 196.
2. Herman, *Trauma and Recovery*, 197.
3. Kanako Taku et al., "The Factor Structure of the Posttraumatic Growth Inventory: A Comparison of Five Models Using Confirmatory Factor Analysis," *Journal of Traumatic Stress* 21, no. 2 (April 2008): 158–164, https://doi.org/10.1002/jts.20305; R. G. Tedeschi and L. G. Calhoun, "The Posttraumatic Growth Inventory: Measuring the Positive Legacy of Trauma," *Journal of Traumatic Stress* 9, no. 3 (July 1996): 455–471, https://doi.org/10.1007/BF02103658.
4. Herman, *Trauma and Recovery*, 211.

CHAPTER FIVE

1. Howard Zehr is often misattributed as being the founder of restorative justice. Zehr himself notes that he has been falsely recognized for this achievement and that credit deserves to be given to Indigenous communities who created and continue to use restorative practices as the cornerstone of their justice systems. See Howard Zehr et al., *The Big Book of Restorative Justice: Four Classic Justice & Peacebuilding Books in One Volume* (Good Books, 2015), 20–1, 56.
2. Sandra Pavelka, "Restorative Justice in the States: An Analysis of Statutory Legislation and Policy," *Justice Policy Journal* 2, no. 13 (Fall 2016): 1–23.

3. For a book-length consideration of how and why schools should use restorative justice, see Katherine Evans and Dorothy Vaandering, *Little Book of Restorative Justice in Education: Fostering Responsibility, Healing, and Hope in Schools* (New York: Good Books, 2016).
4. For but one example of how use of restorative justice brings about lower recidivism rates than the criminal justice system, see David Karp and Casey Sacks, "Student Conduct, Restorative Justice, and Student Development: Findings from the STARR Project: A Student Accountability and Restorative Research Project," *Contemporary Justice Review* 17, no. 2 (June 23, 2014): 154–72, https://doi.org/10.1080/10282580.2014.915140.
5. Danielle Sered, *Until We Reckon: Violence, Mass Incarceration, and a Road to Repair* (New York: The New Press, 2019), 7.
6. United States Sentencing Commission, "Recidivism among Federal Violent Offenders," 3.
7. Sered, *Until We Reckon,* 68–9.
8. For an important study of how trauma permeates the prison system, see James Gilligan, *Violence: Reflections on a National Epidemic* (New York: Vintage, 1997).
9. For a book-length examination of racial injustice in the criminal justice system, see Michelle Alexander, *The New Jim Crow: Mass Incarceration in the Age of Colorblindness* (New York: The New Press, 2012). For a book-length examination of racial bias and restorative justice, see Fania E. Davis, *The Little Book of Race and Restorative Justice: Black Lives, Healing, and US Social Transformation* (New York: Good Books, 2019).
10. For a book-length treatment of the pastoral care of Black men, including how mass incarceration and systemic oppression affects their pastoral needs, see Gregory C. Ellison, *Cut Dead but Still Alive: Caring for African American Young Men* (Nashville: Abingdon Press, 2013).
11. NAACP, "Criminal Justice Fact Sheet," May 24, 2021, https://naacp.org/resources/criminal-justice-fact-sheet.
12. Alexander, *The New Jim Crow*, 205.
13. For a book-length examination of the relationship between restorative justice and race, see Davis, *The Little Book of Race and Restorative Justice.*
14. Jeff Latimer, Craig Dowden, and Danielle Muise, "The Effectiveness of Restorative Justice Practices: A Meta-Analysis," *Government of Canada* Department of Justice (August 11, 2001), https://www.justice.gc.ca/eng/rp-pr/csj-sjc/jsp-sjp/rp01_1-dr01_1/index.html.
15. Sered, *Until We Reckon*, 91–129.
16. Sered, *Until We Reckon*, 92–3.

17. Mary Clark Moschella notes that pastoral theologians may overfocus on care during times of suffering while neglecting to consider how care may also occur in times of joy. While joy may appear to be a state that lacks vulnerability, Brené Brown suggests that vulnerability may profoundly accompany experiences of joy because at such times, the positive feelings people have make them aware that they have much that could be lost should the feeling dissipate. This can lead to fear, acts of self-preservation, or even self-sabotage. See Mary Clark Moschella, *Caring for Joy: Narrative, Theology and Practice* (Boston: Brill Academic Pub, 2016), 2–4; Brené Brown, *Atlas of the Heart: Mapping Meaningful Connection and the Language of Human Experience* (New York: Random House, 2021), 215–216.
18. Justes, *Please Don't Tell*, 29. Here Justes recognizes that active listening, openness, and receptivity on the part of pastoral caregivers creates space for care seekers to regain agency by deciding for themselves what they care to share and what they do not.
19. Doehring, *The Practice of Pastoral Care*, 15–21.
20. Eric Law, "Flowers and Songs: A Liturgical Approach to Pastoral Care," in *Injustice and the Care of Souls: Taking Oppression Seriously in Pastoral Care*, ed. Sheryl A. Kujawa-Holbrook and Karen B. Montagno (Minneapolis: Fortress Press, 2009), 173–183.
21. Herman, *Trauma and Recovery*, 155–174.
22. Herman, *Trauma and Recovery*, 175–214.
23. For an intersectional womanist consideration of how pastoral theology can contribute to racial reconciliation, see Chanequa Walker-Barnes, *I Bring the Voices of My People: A Womanist Vision for Racial Reconciliation* (Grand Rapids, MI: Eerdmans, 2019).
24. For a significant series of articles in the field of pastoral care that offer analyses from an intersectional perspective, see volume 28, issue 3 of the *Journal of Pastoral Theology*, as well as the introduction by editors Lee and Sharp, "Interrogating Identities, Histories, and Cultures" (133–8). For a helpful intersectional introduction to restorative justice principles and practices, see Woolford and Nelund, *The Politics of Restorative Justice: A Critical Introduction*, 2nd ed., particularly pages 152–180.
25. William A. Clebsch and Charles R. Jaekle, eds., *Pastoral Care in Historical Perspective* (Jason Aronson, 1994), 11–32.
26. While Christian communities—particularly the Mennonites—have adopted restorative justice principles into their practices because they align with their theology, Zehr notes that restorative justice primarily emerged in Indigenous communities and was adopted by Christians. Zehr et al., *The Big Book of Restorative Justice*, 20–21, 56.

27. For a helpful introduction to how to use proxies in mediation, see Alissa Ackerman and Jill Levenson, *Healing from Sexual Violence* (Brandon, VT: Safer Society Press, 2009).
28. The University of San Diego runs a series of well-respected restorative justice training geared toward specific contexts. These can be done in person or online via intensive or part-time courses that meet asynchronously or once per week.

CONCLUSION

1. Mary Harvey, *An Ecological View of Psychological Trauma*, unpublished manuscript (Cambridge, MA: Cambridge Hospital, 1990) as cited in Herman, *Trauma and Recovery*, 213.

GLOSSARY

1. Diane Benoit, "Infant-Parent Attachment: Definition, Types, Antecedents, Measurement and Outcome," *Paediatrics & Child Health* 9, no. 8 (October 2004): 541–545.

BIBLIOGRAPHY

Ackerman, Alissa, and Jill Levenson. *Healing from Sexual Violence*. Brandon, VT: Safer Society Press, 2009.

Adams, Marilyn McCord. *Christ and Horrors: The Coherence of Christology*. New York: Cambridge University Press, 2006.

———. *Horrendous Evils and the Goodness of God*. Ithaca: Cornell University Press, 2000.

Agger, Inger, and Søren Buus Jensen. "Testimony as Ritual and Evidence in Psychotherapy for Political Refugees." *Journal of Traumatic Stress* 3, no. 1 (1990): 115–130.

Alexander, Michelle. *The New Jim Crow: Mass Incarceration in the Age of Colorblindness*. New York: The New Press, 2012.

Auden, W. H. *Collected Poems of W. H. Auden*. New York: Vintage, 1991.

Benjet, C., E. Bromet, E. G. Karam, R. C. Kessler, K. A. McLaughlin, A. M. Ruscio, V. Shahly, et al. "The Epidemiology of Traumatic Event Exposure Worldwide: Results from the World Mental Health Survey Consortium." *Psychological Medicine* 46, no. 2 (January 2016): 327–343. https://doi.org/10.1017/S0033291715001981.

Benoit, Diane. "Infant-Parent Attachment: Definition, Types, Antecedents, Measurement and Outcome." *Paediatrics & Child Health* 9, no. 8 (October 2004): 541–545.

Bowler, Kate. *Everything Happens for a Reason: And Other Lies I've Loved*. New York: Random House Trade Paperbacks, 2019.

Brison, Susan J. *Aftermath*. Princeton: Princeton University Press, 2003. https://press.princeton.edu/books/paperback/9780691115702/aftermath.

Brown, Brené. *Atlas of the Heart: Mapping Meaningful Connection and the Language of Human Experience*. New York: Random House, 2021.

Brown, Lily A., Gina M. Belli, Anu Asnaani, and Edna B. Foa. "A Review of the Role of Negative Cognitions About Oneself, Others, and the

World in the Treatment of PTSD." *Cognitive Therapy and Research* 43, no. 1 (February 1, 2019): 143–173. https://doi.org/10.1007/s10608-018-9938-1.

CDC. "Fast Fact: Preventing School Violence," September 2, 2021. https://www.cdc.gov/violenceprevention/youthviolence/schoolviolence/fastfact.html.

———. "Fast Facts: Preventing Child Abuse & Neglect" April 6, 2022. https://www.cdc.gov/violenceprevention/childabuseandneglect/fastfact.html.

Clark, Timothy R. *The 4 Stages of Psychological Safety: Defining the Path to Inclusion and Innovation*. Oakland, CA: Berrett-Koehler Publishers, 2020.

Clebsch, William A., and Charles R. Jaekle, eds. *Pastoral Care in Historical Perspective*. Rev. ed. Jason Aronson, Inc., 1994.

Cooper-White, Pamela. *Gender, Violence, and Justice: Collected Essays on Violence against Women*. Cascade Books, 2019.

Crumpton, Stephanie M. *A Womanist Pastoral Theology Against Intimate and Cultural Violence*. Palgrave Macmillan, 2014.

Davis, Fania E. *The Little Book of Race and Restorative Justice: Black Lives, Healing, and US Social Transformation*. New York: Good Books, 2019.

DeAngelis, Tori. "The Legacy of Trauma: An Emerging Line of Research Is Exploring How Historical and Cultural Trauma Affect Survivors' Children for Generations to Come." *American Psychological Association Monitor* 5, no. 2 (July 3, 2019): 36.

Doehring, Carrie. *The Practice of Pastoral Care: A Postmodern Approach*. Louisville, KY: Westminster John Knox Press, 2006.

Doehring, Carrie, and Allison Kestenbaum. "Interpersonal Competencies for Cultivating Spiritual Trust." In *Chaplaincy and Spiritual Care in the Twenty-First Century* edited by Wendy Cadge and Shelly Rambo, 134–155. Chapel Hill: University of North Carolina Press, 2022. https://uncpress.org/book/9781469667607/chaplaincy-and-spiritual-care-in-the-twenty-first-century/.

Dulmus, Catherine N., and Carolyn Hilarski. "When Stress Constitutes Trauma and Trauma Constitutes Crisis: The Stress-Trauma-Crisis Continuum." *Brief Treatment and Crisis Intervention* 3, no. 1 (2003): 27–35. https://doi.org/10.1093/brief-treatment/mhg008.

Ellison, Gregory C. *Cut Dead but Still Alive: Caring for African American Young Men*. Nashville: Abingdon Press, 2013.

Evans, Katherine, and Dorothy Vaandering. *Little Book of Restorative Justice in Education: Fostering Responsibility, Healing, and Hope in Schools*. New York: Good Books, 2016.

Fadus, Matthew C., Kenneth R. Ginsburg, Kunmi Sobowale, Colleen A. Halliday-Boykins, Brittany E. Bryant, Kevin M. Gray, and Lindsay M. Squeglia. "Unconscious Bias and the Diagnosis of Disruptive Behavior Disorders and ADHD in African American and Hispanic Youth." *Academic Psychiatry* 44, no. 1 (February 1, 2020): 95–102. https://doi.org/10.1007/s40596-019-01127-6.

Figley, Charles R. *Compassion Fatigue: Coping with Secondary Traumatic Stress Disorder in those who Treat the Traumatized.* New York: Brunner-Routledge, 1995.

Fitchett, George. *Assessing Spiritual Needs.* Academic Renewal Press, 2002.

Foa, E. B., and S. P. Cahill. "Psychological Therapies: Emotional Processing." In *International Encyclopedia of the Social & Behavioral Sciences*, edited by Neil J. Smelser and Paul B. Baltes, 12363–12369. Oxford: Pergamon, 2001.

Fromm, M. Gerard. *Lost in Transmission: Studies of Trauma Across Generations.* London: Routledge, 2012.

Gibson, Danjuma. "Christian Triumphalism: The Antithesis to Trauma Recovery." *FORUM: Calvin Seminary Forum* 27, no. 2 (Winter 2020).

Gilligan, James. *Violence: Reflections on a National Epidemic.* New York: Vintage, 1997.

Harvard Medical School. "National Comorbidity Survey," 2005. https://www.hcp.med.harvard.edu/ncs/index.php.

Harvey, Mary. *An Ecological View of Psychological Trauma.* Unpublished manuscript. Cambridge, MA: Cambridge Hospital,, 1990.

Herman, Judith. *Trauma and Recovery: The Aftermath of Violence—From Domestic Abuse to Political Terror.* New York: Basic Books, 1997.

Hout, Wiljo J. P. J. van, and Paul M. G. Emmelkamp. "Exposure in Vivo Therapy." In *Encyclopedia of Psychotherapy*, edited by Michael Hersen and William Sledge, 761–768. Cambridge, MA: Academic Press, 2002.

Hurley, Lawrence. "U.S. Supreme Court Expands State Power over Native American Tribes." *Reuters*, June 30, 2022, sec. United States. https://www.reuters.com/world/us/us-supreme-court-expands-state-power-over-tribes-win-oklahoma-2022-06-29/.

Justes, Emma J. *Hearing Beyond the Words: How to Become a Listening Pastor.* Nashville: Abingdon Press, 2002.

———. *Please Don't Tell: What to Do with the Secrets People Share.* Nashville: Abingdon Press, 2014.

Kahn, William A. "Psychological Conditions of Personal Engagement and Disengagement at Work." *Academy of Management Journal* 33, no. 4 (1990): 692–724.

Karp, David, and Casey Sacks. "Student Conduct, Restorative Justice, and Student Development: Findings from the STARR Project: A Student Accountability and Restorative Research Project." *Contemporary Justice Review* 17, no. 2 (June 23, 2014): 154–172. https://doi.org/10.1080/10282580.2014.915140.

Keep Sweet: Pray and Obey. Netflix, 2022.

Kolk, Bessel A. van der, Laura Stone, Jennifer West, Alison Rhodes, David Emerson, Michael Suvak, and Joseph Spinazzola. "Yoga as an Adjunctive Treatment for Posttraumatic Stress Disorder: A Randomized Controlled Trial." *The Journal of Clinical Psychiatry* 75, no. 6 (June 15, 2014): e559–565. https://doi.org/10.4088/JCP.13m08561.

Kolk, Bessel van der. *The Body Keeps the Score: Brain, Mind, and Body in the Healing of Trauma*. New York: Viking, 2014.

Landreman, Lisa M., ed. *The Art of Effective Facilitation: Reflections From Social Justice Educators*. Sterling, VA,: Stylus Publishing, 2013.

Latimer, Jeff, Craig Dowden, and Danielle Muise. "The Effectiveness of Restorative Justice Practices: A Meta-Analysis." *Government of Canada* Department of Justice (August 11, 2001). https://www.justice.gc.ca/eng/rp-pr/csj-sjc/jsp-sjp/rp01_1-dr01_1/index.html.

Laub, Dori, and Shoshana Felman. *Testimony: Crises of Witnessing in Literature, Psychoanalysis and History*. London: Routledge, 1991. https://www.routledge.com/Testimony-Crises-of-Witnessing-in-Literature-Psychoanalysis-and-History/Felman-Laub/p/book/9780415903929.

Law, Eric. "Flowers and Songs: A Liturgical Approach to Pastoral Care." In *Injustice and the Care of Souls: Taking Oppression Seriously in Pastoral Care*, edited by Sheryl A. Kujawa-Holbrook and Karen B. Montagno, 173–183. Minneapolis: Fortress Press, 2009.

Lee, K. Samuel, and Melinda A. McGarrah Sharp. "Interrogating Identities, Histories, and Cultures: Intersectional Pastoral Theology and Care." *Journal of Pastoral Theology* 28, no. 3 (September 2, 2018): 133–138. https://doi.org/10.1080/10649867.2018.1562659.

Leslie, Kristen J. *When Violence Is No Stranger: Pastoral Counseling with Survivors of Acquaintance Rape*. Minneapolis: Fortress Press, 2002.

Loewenberg, Peter. "Clinical and Historical Perspectives on the Intergenerational Transmission of Trauma." In *Lost in Transmission: Studies of Trauma Across Generations*, edited by M. Gerard Fromm. London: Routledge, 2012.

Machado, Carmen Maria. *Her Body and Other Parties*. Minneapolis: Graywolf Press, 2017.

McCarroll, Pamela R., ed. *The End of Hope—The Beginning: Narratives of Hope in the Face of Death and Trauma*. Minneapolis: Fortress Press, 2014.

Merrick, Melissa T. "Vital Signs: Estimated Proportion of Adult Health Problems Attributable to Adverse Childhood Experiences and Implications for Prevention—25 States, 2015–2017." *MMWR. Morbidity and Mortality Weekly Report* 68 (2019). https://doi.org/10.15585/mmwr.mm6844e1.

Miller, Chanel. *Know My Name*. New York: Penguin Random House, 2019.

Moschella, Mary Clark. *Caring for Joy: Narrative, Theology and Practice*. Boston: Brill Academic Pub, 2016.

NAACP. "Criminal Justice Fact Sheet," May 24, 2021. https://naacp.org/resources/criminal-justice-fact-sheet

Osofsky, Joy D., Putnam, Frank W., & Lederman, Cindy S. "How to Maintain Emotional Health when Working with Trauma." *Juvenile and Family Court Journal*, 59, no. 4 (Fall, 2008), 91–102.

Ozer, Emily J., Suzanne R. Best, Tami L. Lipsey, and Daniel S. Weiss. "Predictors of Posttraumatic Stress Disorder and Symptoms in Adults: A Meta-Analysis." *Psychological Bulletin* 129, no. 1 (January 2003): 52–73. https://doi.org/10.1037/0033-2909.129.1.52.

Pargament, Kenneth I., ed. *APA Handbook of Psychology, Religion, and Spirituality*. Washington, DC: American Psychological Association, 2013.

———. *The Psychology of Religion and Coping: Theory, Research, Practice*. Rev. ed. New York: The Guilford Press, 2001.

Pargament, Kenneth I., and Julie J. Exline. *Working with Spiritual Struggles in Psychotherapy: From Research to Practice*. New York: The Guilford Press, 2021.

Pargament, Kenneth I., Margaret Feuille, and Donna Burdzy. "The Brief RCOPE: Current Psychometric Status of a Short Measure of Religious Coping." *Religions* 2, no. 1 (March 2011): 51–76. https://doi.org/10.3390/rel2010051.

Pargament, Kenneth I., Harold G. Koenig, Nalini Tarakeshwar, and June Hahn. "Religious Coping Methods as Predictors of Psychological, Physical and Spiritual Outcomes among Medically Ill Elderly Patients: A Two-Year Longitudinal Study." *Journal of Health Psychology* 9, no. 6 (November 2004): 713–730. https://doi.org/10.1177/1359105304045366.

Park, Crystal L., and Ian A. Gutierrez. "Global and Situational Meanings in the Context of Trauma: Relations with Psychological Well-Being." *Counselling Psychology Quarterly* 26, no. 1 (March 1, 2013): 8–25. https://doi.org/10.1080/09515070.2012.727547.

Park, Crystal L. "Distinctions to Promote an Integrated Perspective on Meaning: Global Meaning and Meaning-Making Processes." *Journal of Constructivist Psychology* 30, no. 1 (January 2, 2017): 14–19. https://doi.org/10.1080/10720537.2015.1119082.

———. "Making Sense of the Meaning Literature: An Integrative Review of Meaning Making and Its Effects on Adjustment to Stressful Life Events." *Psychological Bulletin* 136, no. 2 (March 2010): 257–301. https://doi.org/10.1037/a0018301.

———. "Meaning Making Following Trauma." *Frontiers in Psychology* 13 (March 23, 2022): 844891. https://doi.org/10.3389/fpsyg.2022.844891.

Park, Crystal L., Kristen E. Riley, Login S. George, Ian A. Gutierrez, Amy E. Hale, Dalnim Cho, and Tosca D. Braun. "Assessing Disruptions in Meaning: Development of the Global Meaning Violation Scale." *Cognitive Therapy and Research* 40, no. 6 (December 1, 2016): 831–846. https://doi.org/10.1007/s10608-016-9794-9.

Patel, Anushka R., and Brian J. Hall. "Beyond the DSM-5 Diagnoses: A Cross-Cultural Approach to Assessing Trauma Reactions." *FOCUS* 19, no. 2 (June 2021): 197–203. https://doi.org/10.1176/appi.focus.20200049.

Pavelka, Sandra. "Restorative Justice in the States: An Analysis of Statutory Legislation and Policy." *Justice Policy Journal* 2, no. 13 (Fall 2016): 1–23.

Ramsay, Nancy, and Carrie Doehring, eds. *Military Moral Injury and Spiritual Care: A Resource for Religious Leaders and Professional Caregivers.* Chalice Press, 2019.

Robins, Rochelle, and Danielle Tumminio Hansen. "Meaning Making Through Ritual and Public Leadership." In *Chaplaincy and Spiritual Care in the Twenty-First Century: An Introduction*, edited by Wendy Cadge and Shelly Rambo, 110–125. Chapel Hill: University of North Carolina Press, 2022.

Rogers-Vaughn, Bruce. *Caring for Souls in a Neoliberal Age.* New York: Palgrave Macmillan, 2016.

Schnurr, Paula P. "Epidemiology and Impact of PTSD—PTSD: National Center for PTSD." US Department of Veteran Affairs. Accessed January 23, 2023. https://www.ptsd.va.gov/professional/treat/essentials/epidemiology.asp.

Sered, Danielle. *Until We Reckon: Violence, Mass Incarceration, and a Road to Repair.* New York: The New Press, 2019.

Smith, Gregory A. "About Three-in-Ten U.S. Adults Are Now Religiously Unaffiliated." *Pew Research Center's Religion & Public Life Project* (blog), December 14, 2021. https://www.pewresearch.org/religion/2021/12/14/about-three-in-ten-u-s-adults-are-now-religiously-unaffiliated/.

Southern Poverty Law Center. "Fundamentalist Church of Jesus Christ of Latter-Day Saints." Accessed February 11, 2023.

https://www.splcenter.org/fighting-hate/extremist-files/group/fundamentalist-church-jesus-christ-latter-day-saints.

Swinton, John. *Raging with Compassion: Pastoral Responses to the Problem of Evil*. Grand Rapids, MI: Eerdmans, 2007.

Taku, Kanako, Arnie Cann, Lawrence G. Calhoun, and Richard G. Tedeschi. "The Factor Structure of the Posttraumatic Growth Inventory: A Comparison of Five Models Using Confirmatory Factor Analysis." *Journal of Traumatic Stress* 21, no. 2 (April 2008): 158–164. https://doi.org/10.1002/jts.20305.

Tedeschi, R. G., and L. G. Calhoun. "The Posttraumatic Growth Inventory: Measuring the Positive Legacy of Trauma." *Journal of Traumatic Stress* 9, no. 3 (July 1996): 455–471. https://doi.org/10.1007/BF02103658.

Trevino, Kelly M., Kenneth I. Pargament, Neal Krause, Gail Ironson, and Peter Hill. "Stressful Events and Religious/Spiritual Struggle: Moderating Effects of the General Orienting System." *Psychology of Religion and Spirituality* 11 (2019): 214–224. https://doi.org/10.1037/rel0000149.

Tumminio Hansen, Danielle. *Conceiving Family: A Practical Theology of Surrogacy and Self.* Waco, TX: Baylor University Press, 2019.

———. "Restorative Justice and Pastoral Care: Shared Principles and Practices." *Journal of Pastoral Theology*. February 6, 2024. https://doi.org/10.1080/10649867.2023.2294630

———. *Speaking of Rape: The Limits of Language in Sexual Violations*. Minneapolis: Fortress Press, 2024.

Tumminio Hansen, Danielle Elizabeth. "The Body of God, Sexually Violated: A Trauma-Informed Reading of the Climate Crisis." *Religions* 13, no. 3 (March 2022): 249–261. https://doi.org/10.3390/rel13030249.

United States Sentencing Commission. "Recidivism Among Federal Violent Offenders," January 23, 2019. https://www.ussc.gov/research/research-reports/recidivism-among-federal-violent-offenders.

US Department of Health and Human Services. "Understanding Child Trauma." Accessed January 24, 2023. https://www.samhsa.gov/child-trauma/understanding-child-trauma.

Walker-Barnes, Chanequa. *I Bring the Voices of My People: A Womanist Vision for Racial Reconciliation*. Grand Rapids, MI: Eerdmans, 2019.

Woolford, Andrew, and Amanda Nelund. *The Politics of Restorative Justice: A Critical Introduction, Second Edition*. Boulder, CO: Lynne Rienner Publishers, 2020.

Zehr, Howard, Allan MacRae, Kay Pranis, and Lorraine Stutzman Amstutz. *The Big Book of Restorative Justice: Four Classic Justice & Peacebuilding Books in One Volume*. Good Books, 2015.

INDEX